And I Will DECLARE HIS GREATNESS

Stories of God's
Goodness and Faithfulness
through Answered Prayer

JEANIE SELBY

And I Will Declare His Greatness:
Stories of God's Goodness and Faithfulness through Answered Prayer

Copyright ©2023 by Jeanie Selby

All rights reserved.

No part of this publication may be reproduced, stored in a retrieval system, or transmitted in any form or by any means—electronic, mechanical, photocopy, recording, or any other—without the prior permission of the author.

Scripture quotations from The Authorized (King James) Version. Rights in the Authorized Version in the United Kingdom are vested in the Crown. Reproduced by permission of the Crown's patentee, Cambridge University Press.

Paperback ISBN: 978-1-950685-93-6
E-book ISBN: 978-1-950685-99-8
Library of Congress Control Number: 2023905387

Printed in the USA

*And men shall speak of the might of thy terrible acts:
and I will declare thy greatness.*
—*Psalm 145:6*

Contents

Introduction vii

Please Put Me On Someone's Heart 1
God Is Right On Time 3
Wait Upon The Lord 6
Where Could I Go But To The Lord 9
God's Grace On Gracie 11
Mommy, Please Come Home 20
Lord, Please Help That Lady 25
You Can't Outsmart God 28
God Owns It All 31
God Knows Our Every Need 35
Oh Lord, This Family Needs You 39
Wherever He Leads, I'll Go 44
Oh, To Know Your Voice 47
Lord, I Can't Do This 49
God, You Are Amazing 52
Acknowledge Him And Him Only 59
Going Home 65
Listen To Your Momma 75
Who Was The Other Person 77
It's Only Six Dollars Over 80
Why Won't You Heal Me? 83
God And Alcohol Don't Mix 88

Just As I Am 94
God Knows The Desire Of Your Heart 99
God, I Don't Have A Dollar Left To My Name 103
God Made All Things New 105
It's Your Child, So You Pray 113
God Never Ceases To Amaze Me 116
Saddest Day Of My Life 119
God Will Protect And Provide 122
Tested, Tried, And True 126
God, Please Stop Her From Drowning 129
Mom, Were You Praying For Me? 132
Why Don't You Ask God For A Winter Coat 135
If I Die Before You Come Back, Just Know I Went To Heaven 138
Happy Anniversary 142
The Greatest Gift Is To Pray 147
When The Walls Start Crashing In 151
When We Are Foolish, He Is Faithful 154
God Help Me 158

Acknowledgments 161
About the Author 163

Introduction

When I asked the Lord to come into my life to live and fix my brokenness, I never dreamed He would use me for His service in any way. I was such a failure; I guess I broke every commandment that was ever written—and then some. I now can only dream of what He could have done with my life. If only I had understood His love for me, and if only I had been taught the power of prayer and being obedient to His Word at a young age, I just thank God we are never too old to learn.

Alone one night in my living room, I asked God to help me to know His voice. I said, "Lord, You say, 'My sheep hear My voice, and they follow Me.' How can I know it is Your voice I am hearing?" The closer I got to Christ through reading His Word, praying, and attending a Bible-believing church, the more He started changing my mind and life's situations, and the more I wanted others to experience what God was capable of doing in their life as well. This book is about how a perfect God can take an imperfect person and use them for His glory. It is a book that I pray will give hope to anyone who stopped believing that God answers prayers. I trust you will start believing and praying without ceasing until the answer comes. It is my heart's desire that you will give God every situation in your life, and you will be humbled at the glory of His presence as you seek Him with all your heart.

For it is a journey that only you can go on alone. He wants to be your personal Lord and Savior. Although many will influence you along the way, it will be what you do with and for Christ that will get you through each and every day of your life.

Father, may nothing but Your greatness be seen in the pages to follow. I pray You will protect the heart of each reader and give them the desire to crave Your will in their lives. I pray You change and use them for Your glory. Amen.

THE WISDOM OF CHRIST—WITHOUT WORKING FOR CHRIST—IS WORTHLESS.

Please Put Me On Someone's Heart

When you are trying to pray and are heavily burdened, do you get a sense that your prayers are not hitting the ceiling? I had heard that said many times in my life but never had experienced it until one day, alone in my living room, I was praying about a situation that was getting worse by the day. Although I truly do not remember now what I was praying about that day, I do know I was in tears, crying out for God to change the situation. I remember feeling scared and helpless and felt a heavy void in my praying. I did not like the heaviness my heart was feeling, and I sure didn't like the loneliness I felt as I cried out to God.

Soon a thought crossed my mind: *Just stop. Your prayers are not being heard; they are not even hitting the ceiling.* In defeat, I cried out and said, "Father God, will you please put me on someone's heart to pray for me?!"

Now, I don't know if I really believed He would do what I had just asked, but I do know that I felt a great void between myself and God. Little did I know, I was about to find out just how much He knew my every thought.

All week long, I would think of praying but thought maybe God didn't have time for me. Can you imagine thinking that God isn't interested in listening to you? Well, that is exactly how I felt. I've come across a few people who have felt the same way and have even stopped believing that there is a God because He didn't answer their prayers as they thought He should have.

At the end of the week, I was going on visitation with Sherry, a classmate from my Sunday school class. We were visiting a lady who had missed a few weeks of church, and we wanted to make sure she was doing okay.

When we arrived at her house, she welcomed our visit and was glad we came by. She said she had been fine but was going through a family crisis that she had to work through. We talked about all that was going on in her life's situation and then prayed for her, asking God to work everything out.

Sherry and I then walked back to the car to leave, but as I was about to get in the car, the lady asked if I would come back for a minute, so I walked back onto her porch. As I approached her, she said, "Jeanie, I couldn't let you leave without telling you that God put you on my heart this week, and I have been praying for you." Oh, how thankful I was that she didn't let me leave before telling me that our God had put me on her heart to pray for me!

I have never again had any doubt that God hears and cares when I cry out to Him. I may not understand why He hasn't answered when I thought He should have, but I have never doubted that my prayers are heard.

There have been many times that I've had to ask God to show me sin in my life that might be stopping Him from answering my prayer or a situation in my life that I need to take care of, and He is always ready to show me. That day, He showed me very clearly that He hears my every word. Even if I don't think He is listening, I just have to remember that wonderful day, and all doubt is gone.

We serve an awesome God! He knows our hearts, and He hears our every prayer.

Satan is fighting for your disbelief in prayer. He really doesn't care if you go to church, sing in the choir, or even go on visitation as long as you don't pray.

Lord God Almighty, Thank you for the privilege to come to the Throne of Grace.

> *And this is the confidence that we have in him, that, if we ask any thing according to his will, he heareth us.*
> *—1 John 5:14*

GOD IS RIGHT ON TIME

It seemed our whole married life Gary and I were trying to get ahead. There never seemed to be enough money or time to go around. God showed us over and over that He was the supplier of all our needs and we would always have enough. But only after being taught the truth did our perspective change.

One Sunday morning, Pastor Steve started a three-month series on the biblical truth of giving. I know—everyone hates that message, but can I tell you it was a life changer for us. I suppose there are many ministers who tiptoe around the tithing messages—probably afraid of the backlash of either unsigned rebuttal letters or people just leaving the church in disobedience—but I can truly say those messages were life-changing for us. And just for the record, the church experienced the largest growth in families joining the church in that quarter of tithing sermons than any other quarter for many years.

Tithing involves completely trusting the Lord. That was a lesson I had down pat—WRONG! I gave my 10 percent faithfully unless something major came up, and then I just knew God would understand if I took care of the situation with the tithing money and played catch up next week—which seldom ever happened.

Then came the day that Pastor Steve preached on Malachi 3:8–11. "Will a man rob God? Yet ye have robbed me. But ye say, Wherein have we robbed thee? In tithes and offerings. Ye are cursed with a curse: for ye have robbed me, even this whole nation." WHAT? I had never heard of or read that before. Truly, the reason I gave a tenth at all was because my mother said we were supposed to, and that was okay with me. But thinking of all the times I had robbed Him was horrible. *Wow, God, please forgive me.* Then I thought of the times I didn't tithe because I thought I might need it, and sure enough, something would happen. Many things were racing through my mind; I felt so bad. I had to change my way of thinking. Malachi 3:10 says, "Bring ye all the tithes into the storehouse, that there may be meat in my house, and prove me now herewith, saith the Lord of host, if I will not open the windows of heaven, and pour you out a blessing, that there shall not be room enough to receive it." *Prove me.* Pastor Steve said God was saying to put Him to the test and see if He won't supply your needs. Oh my—now, that thought really scared me. When I got home, I looked up the word *prove*. I saw that God was also saying, "It is true; it is the case."

I then realized that my way of looking at the things of God was going to change that day. I started praying for God to help me to trust Him in every aspect of my life and to protect me from attacks from Satan because He said in verse 11: "And I will rebuke the devourer for your sakes, and he shall not destroy the fruits of your ground; neither shall your vine cast her fruit before her time in the field, saith the Lord of hosts." To me, that was my assurance that if I was faithful to God, He would supply all my needs.

I was put to the test very quickly. I remember we had three bills that needed to be paid, and I did not have the money. I was barely making ends meet. I was trying my best to pray and give God our finances, but I felt like a big failure. I thought that I probably had things too messed up for God to be able to fix at that time. Those bills had to be paid on Friday, and all week I was asking God to show me what to do. I felt like I was asking Him to pull money out of thin air and place it in my hands as I stood there begging. I went to the store to get a few things, and I remember thinking, *What are you doing here? You need to go home and make do with what you have.* I started crying, then went to my car and just broke down. I prayed some more and said, "Lord, You said You would supply all my needs, and I believe You will. If these bills don't get paid, then I am going to believe we don't need them, and I accept that, and I thank You." I went home and started fixing dinner with my daughter Montana at the counter helping me. I don't know if she sensed something was wrong or not—if she did, she wouldn't say anything—but she would try to help. We were working in silence when a hand came from behind and placed a check in front of my face. It was exactly the amount we needed for those bills, not a penny more or less. And again, I couldn't do anything but break down and cry, but this time it was tears of joy and thankfulness, rejoicing that our God is not a God of coincidence but a God of commitment.

Where did the money come from, you might ask. Well, Gary had just started working a new job selling insurance, and he received monthly checks starting out. As a result, we had to make adjustments with providing extra gas money, new clothes, and many other things besides the regular household and family needs. That check was his first commission check. He was not expecting a check that day, but God knew the very day it was to be sent. He knew when we would need it. God is right on time!

Father God Almighty, may we find it in our hearts to believe You know our every need with the same faith we believed You to save us, and may we give You the power over our finances to do as You please. And may we experience the joy of Your will in our lives by doing so. Amen.

> *Humble yourselves therefore under the mighty hand of God, that he may exalt you in due time: Casting all your care upon him; for he careth for you.*
> —1 Peter 5:6–7

WAIT UPON THE LORD

There I was, sitting at my daughter's softball game when a thought came to me to go home and call Patty. I just ignored the thought and kept watching the game because I was not about to leave my daughter's game to call a friend for no reason—or so I thought. *Go call Patty* would not leave my mind. It was so powerful I knew I better go call her. So as hard as it was for me to leave, I knew in my heart it was something I had to do. I told my husband, Gary, that I would be right back, I had to make a phone call, and the look on his face was one of WHY? I didn't know for sure. All I knew was when a thought wouldn't leave me, God was speaking, and I had learned to obey.

Patty is a friend and, at that time, was in her early twenties. She was helping her family in a business they owned in town, she was still living with her parents, but she wanted to find a place to call her own. She had expressed to me her desires, but she felt it was an impossible dream. I asked her if she was praying, asking God if it was His will for her life, and if so, asking Him to find that home for her. She said she had not prayed, nor did she think God would be interested in that part of her life. She didn't really believe you should pray for things like a house or car—you know, material things.

I told Patty that when God saves us, He wants to also save us from making bad choices, so by coming to Him first with all our needs, we are allowing Him to show us His great, powerful love and presence. More than anything, I wanted Patty to not just trust God but obey Him also. I mean, how do you do one without the other?

She said she was a Christian but had never really depended on God to help her; she didn't think He cared what kind of car she drove or what house she lived in. In fact, she didn't think you bothered Almighty God with such frivolous things! I told her God did not look at those things as petty; they were major decisions, and He wanted to be a part of them. So she said she would start praying about a home, and I started praying for her home and for her complete surrender to the Lord.

When I got home, I called Patty and asked what she was doing. She said she was fixing to go out the door to meet a lady and look at an apartment that she had for rent. I told her that I was excited for her and would be praying. Patty said, "Well, I will have to give up my car to be able to afford it, but that will be okay, I guess." I said, "Oh, Patty, you can't do that; how will you get to work at one in the morning? How will you get groceries? You need a car, and if you give up your car, you will be miserable. Patty, we are praying for you a home you can afford, not one you have to give up your car for. Listen, God knows your desire, and if it is His will for you, He is able to provide a home you can afford. You need to trust Him and wait upon Him. I wish you would think this over." Patty went on to say that $300 was about the going rate for apartments around our area. She continued to say it was pretty close to work, and she could borrow her parents' car after work to pay bills and buy groceries. I said, "Patty, there is so much more to it than that. What about the shopping trips at Jonesboro, going out to eat, and trips to the video store? The most important thing of all is you are not waiting on the Lord to provide. I know you are missing out on a blessing to see that He really does care about these areas of your life. I wish you would pray about this." Then she said, "Well, it's too late now. I was supposed to have met the lady thirty minutes ago. I was headed out the door when you called, and she told me not to be late." Again, thank You, Lord!

Two days later, Patty called me and said, "Guess what? I was driving down a street and saw a for rent sign, I called the phone number, met the landlord, and I have just rented an apartment for $150 a month!" She said it was small but perfect for her. She was so proud to have found a place of her own with the help of the Lord. Patty had her eyes opened that day to see the love of God and to give Him everything, for He truly does care for us.

The story doesn't end there. I don't remember just how long it was that Patty lived in the apartment when the landlord asked her if she would like to move into a brick house on the corner for the same amount of rent. She just wanted good renters, and she knew Patty would be perfect by the way she cared for her apartment. And move she did.

And to think she was fixing to walk out the door when I called. Thank You, Lord, for Your sweet voice and the power behind it.

> *Wait on the Lord: be of good courage, and he shall strengthen thine heart: wait, I say, on the Lord.*
> *—Psalm 27:14*

Where Could I Go But To The Lord

Gary and I were living in Enid, Mississippi, and working in Sardis, Mississippi, which was about a thirty-minute drive from our house. The road to our house was long and hilly once you pulled into our subdivision. In fact, if you came down our dead-end road, you were either lost or really knew where we lived. It was 1983, and our phone was on a party line, not something I used too often, so I didn't call home much. We were backwoods folks—on our own except for a few country dogs that would venture down our road to see the girls and get fed. A couple times a year, the owners across the road would come for the weekend. Other than that, there was no one within hollering distance, but we loved that peaceful place—another blessing of God that I will share in another story.

You know, God has His way of meeting us in a valley just so we can see Him in all of His glory, so we can see Him work and build our faith, letting us know that He never leaves us or forsakes us. He also teaches us great lessons in that valley; that is the part I cherish the most, the lessons learned.

One day after work, we had just picked up the girls and pulled in at the house when our oldest daughter cried out, "The car is on fire!" Smoke was rolling out from under the hood of our Plymouth Valiant. Gary popped open the hood and didn't see a fire, so he turned to walk away out of frustration. But before walking away, he looked at me and said, "I guess you are going to pray now," and I said, "Yes, I am!" We were in a bad situation. I am not kidding—maybe you have been there. We didn't know anyone around our home; we had another car under the carport that was far beyond empty in gas, and we were thinking we would need to haul some gas to it in a gas can before trying to move it. And we were broke—not a penny to our name. The next day was Friday and payday, and both our cars were now empty of fuel or smoking.

I started crying and praying for God to help us and show us what to do since we didn't even have family close by. All of a sudden, I realized that I better get out of the smoking car I was still sitting in. I looked up, and there was Gary at the mailbox with a strange look on his face. I got out of the car and walked toward him, wondering what the bad news was he was holding in his hand.

When I joined him at the mailbox, he handed me a letter and a check for twenty-three dollars. Our insurance company sent the check saying they overcharged us. I could tell Gary was taken aback by what had just happened. While God was working on Gary's heart, I was getting the keys to the Buick and fixing to drive that car to an old country store and gas station, one I'd never been to before since the gas was always higher than in town. I was not sure the car had enough gas to make it, but for some reason, I just knew God was going to get me to the store—and He did.

Before I went into the store, I thanked God for getting me there without running out of gas, but now I needed Him to prepare the store owner's heart to cash the check from the insurance company so I could fill our car up—and He did. I can tell you my drive home was full of praises unto my wonderful Savior. I thanked Him for His love and protection—yes, it was shouting time! I know that day made an impact on Gary's life, and it wasn't very long after that he asked the Lord to save him.

Think about it . . . where could I go but to the Lord? Father God and Protector, if there is just one who needs Your help at the time they are reading this story, please take care of them, and may it change their life forever. Amen.

> *God is our refuge and strength,*
> *a very present help in trouble.*
> —*Psalm 46:1*

GOD'S GRACE ON GRACIE

You never know who God has waiting on you to plant a seed in their life. Then there are those He really blesses you with to bring them to full bloom. So it was to be the day He put Gracie in my life.

I was working and was sent to see a lady who was living with her son. Her name was Gracie, and I loved her from the first time I laid eyes on her. She was a short, little-built lady with a long braid hanging down her back. She had the sweetest smile and loved to talk and ask questions. Gracie made me laugh, she was so kind, and she had an innocence about her that was so cute. After we visited a while and got to know each other better, I told her we had better get her a bath and wash her hair.

We walked past the kitchen on our way to the bathroom, and I noticed a towel hanging on a clothesline on the back porch through the open back door. Cigarette smoke was coming through the screen door, so I knew she was not alone.

The talking did not stop as we were getting her shower. It was like she was starved for conversation. After we completed her care, I noticed that there was no place to hang her towels, so I asked if it would be okay for me to hang her towels on the clothesline on the back porch. She looked at me and said, "I got me a machine that will pound and wrench them clothes at the same time." I got so tickled when she said that, and then she said, "You don't believe me, do ya? Come here in the kitchen, and I'll show ya." So I followed her to the kitchen, and there was the washing machine, currently on the spin cycle. Still tickled by her innocence and looking at her standing as far away as she could get from the washer, I asked her if she knew how to work it. "No, but I listen, and I promise, that machine will pound and wrench them clothes at the same time!"

The more we talked, the more I realized that Gracie was so innocent of things in the world. You could tell by her stories she'd lived a hard life, not asking for a thing, not knowing there was anything to ask for, and just doing the best with what she had. She had never seen a washing machine, for crying out loud! Every visit, I left anticipating our next. Not sure how much time she had, I wanted to make her laugh and feel special—because she was. Cancer was growing on the outside of her neck, and though no one knows the hour, I wanted to make my time with her memorable.

As I was getting ready to leave one day, Gracie asked me when she would be seeing me again. I said, "Well, if the Lord comes, I will see you in heaven; if not, I will see you Wednesday."

She then replied, "You going there?"

I asked, "Where?"

And she said, "Heaven."

"Yes, I'm going there."

And she asked, "How?"

"By the blood of Jesus. Gracie, do you know Jesus?"

She hung her head and said no.

"Gracie, would you like to know Jesus?" I asked.

"Yes," she replied.

So I told her I had to go out to the car and I would be right back to tell her how much Jesus loves her. I went to get a Gideons Bible, praying all the way: "God, she does not know You. Please help me. Gracie needs you, and I need You to help me tell this eighty-eight-year-old how much You love her, so she will fully understand. Thank You."

As I entered the house, she had a kitchen chair pulled up right next to her recliner for me to sit in. Then she looked at the book I was holding and said with great reverence, "Is that the Holy Bible?"

"Oh, Lord," I cried out in my heart, "please forgive me for cutting the word 'Holy' off the name of Your Good Book." I told her that it was the Holy Bible, and I was going to read to her just how much Jesus loves her, so she must believe everything I read to be true. I told her if she had any questions to please ask and I would try my best to explain.

In the beginning God created the heavens and the earth. Gracie believed every story I told her, listening with excitement, literally on the edge of her seat—until it came to the virgin birth. She fell back into her seat and said, "Can't no virgin have a baby!"

I said, "No, they cannot, but God needed a womb to carry the baby Jesus; Jesus needed a mother to care for Him, and that is the way God chose to do it. Nothing is impossible with God, and we find that out as we learn to walk and talk with Him daily."

She couldn't get past the understanding of the virgin birth, so I went to the death and resurrection of our Lord Jesus and why He suffered and died a horrible death so that she could be free, and she believed it all. I asked Gracie if she would like to pray and ask Jesus to forgive her of her sins and give her eternal life, and she said so sweetly, "Oh, honey, I haven't done no sin."

And if I didn't know better, I would guess she hadn't sinned at all; you just had to know her. So I showed her in the Holy Bible, Romans 3:23–24: "For all have sinned, and come short of the glory of God; Being justified freely by His grace through the redemption that is in Christ Jesus." I continued, "You see, Gracie, He died to justify us freely. He took our sins on that cross so that we can live as if we have never sinned, and our sins are forgiven if we ask Him to forgive us. Would you like to ask Him to forgive you?

"I better not," she replied.

I could not believe my ears. Then I heard a loud voice say, "You don't need to get her riled up!" I turned around, and it was her son standing behind me, red-faced and mad as thunder. Not one time had I ever seen him, as he stayed on the back porch. I looked him straight in the eyes and said, "Gracie asked to know about Jesus, so I told her. She has a right to know." With that being said, he stormed out of the house.

I asked Gracie again if she would like to ask Jesus into her heart, and she said, "No, I could never pay Him or do anything for Him, and I can't read." Again I reminded her it is not anything we do; it is what He has done for us, and no amount of work on our part can save us. God knew she couldn't read, and that is why He sent me to tell her how much He loves her.

Thinking I would see Gracie in a few days, I left her by saying, "If you decide that you want to ask Jesus into your heart, just tell Him you believe what I told you is true, that He died and rose again, and you are asking Him to forgive you of your sins and come into your heart and save you so you can live with Him forever."

She said thank you, and I left.

When I got in my car, I broke into tears and cried out to God, "Lord, I did my part; now You have to do Yours. Please convict that little heart as only You can. And I pray for her son, Lord; he needs You also." I really could not believe that Gracie would not ask Christ into her life. I was so upset. I drove by Gary's insurance office, and, seeing he was there, I went inside and told him what had just happened. I needed prayers for Gracie.

It was Wednesday morning, and I could not wait to see Gracie. I knocked on the door expecting to see her face, but it was not Gracie's face that I saw—it was her son's. He took one look at me and started shutting the door while yelling, "SHE'S NOT HERE!"

Crazy as I can get sometimes, I put my foot and body against the door, so he could not close the door and asked, "Where is she?"

"She doesn't live here anymore!" he replied while pushing against the door to close it.

"Where does she live?" I cried out, pushing just as hard as he was. I was thinking, *What in the world are you doing, girl?* And I could feel the pressure on my foot, but he answered back.

"Piggott!"

"Where in Piggott?" I asked.

With one last shove that almost broke my foot while shutting the door for good, he said, "By a store!"

I cried out, "What store?" but the door was closed by that time, and he did not answer me.

I went back to my workplace and asked the nurse where Gracie had moved to. They had no idea she had moved at all! After looking into it, all they could find out was she had moved in with her daughter, and the daughter didn't need any help caring for Gracie at that time. No address, no phone number, just a throbbing foot and a broken heart!

A few months later, Gary reminded me that he had a dinner scheduled for his clients at Piggott and let me know what restaurant it would be at and the time he was leaving. I was not going to be able to ride with him because I would not be off work in time, but I told him I would arrive as soon as I could.

After work, I went home to get ready, not one time thinking about Gracie being in Piggott—that is, not until I got in my car when the thought came to my mind and would not leave. Over and over, the thought came to me to go find Gracie. I had thirty miles of fighting the ridiculous thought that was going over and over in my mind. I finally said, "God, I am not going to go find Gracie; there is just no way I can do that. I don't even know what store she lives by, and who's to say her son was telling me the truth. I truly do believe You are wanting me to do this, but I just can't. It is too crazy. I mean, what store, Lord? Do You see what I am saying? Maybe I can find out more information on her whereabouts and go then, but not today, Lord." Even though I felt the Lord was telling me to go, I just could not bring myself to believe it was really what He wanted me to do.

Finally, I made it to the restaurant. I was enjoying visiting with Gary's clients, and I never once thought of Gracie, even though the thought of her consumed my mind every second of the thirty-mile drive there. I felt like I was in a battle, and I guess you could say I was.

After everyone left the dinner, I helped Gary clean up and get his car packed before leaving, still not once thinking of Gracie—that is, not until I started walking to my car. Gary said he would follow me home, and I got into the car to let him do just that, but the thought came back to my mind. I said, out loud, "Lord, what store would I even go to?" and as well as I was sitting there, the words THE FIRST STORE YOU COME TO came to my mind.

So I got out of my car and walked back to Gary and said, "Babe, do you remember the little lady I told you about that would not accept Jesus as her Savior, and I came to your office so upset, then the next week I told you she moved by a store here in Piggott?"

Gary said yes.

"Well, I have got to go find her and tell her about Jesus one more time."

Gary gave me that look, letting me know that the thought was nuts, and he said, "Babe, it is getting late; get in the car and let me follow you home. Besides, what store are you going to go to?"

Bursting into tears, I replied, "The first store I come to!" He knew there was no stopping me. He did offer to go with me, but I knew his heart was not in it, so he went home. I pulled out onto the road, and there was a grocery store on the right with a subdivision next to it, and that is where I pulled in and gave it all to God. I prayed and asked Him to let me know if and when I should go home. It was in the summer, so I had about an hour of daylight left. I sure didn't want to be knocking on doors late at night, but down deep, I was hoping to see Gracie again. I said, "Lord, I am willing, but I am afraid. Please be with me no matter what the outcome. I just want to be Your servant."

Starting on the end of the first street, my plan was to ask the residents in the end houses of each block if they had seen a little lady about four foot ten inches on a walker, living with her daughter, whose name I did not know. So I started on the end of block one, skipped to block two since I was on the end, and then on the last block, I went to the other end and started back to block one. No one had seen the little lady and knew nothing about a lady on their block taking in their mother to care for her. I was finally back to block one, it was a little past nine, and there was one house on the end because the house across the street was empty. When the lady told me she had not seen anyone, I thought there was no need to go to the house beside the empty one. My goodness, the lady across the street just said she hadn't seen my sweet little Gracie.

So I got back in my car and said, "Lord, I really felt that this is what you wanted me to do, so I did it, and Gracie is not here. I don't know what else I can do. I truly did try. I am sorry. I sure thought this was Your will." I got done praying, and I thought, *I know this sounds crazy, but I will feel so much better if I finish off this neighborhood by going to the house next to the empty one,* and so I did. I knocked on the door, gave the lady my search story, and she said, "Yes! Gracie's daughter was my neighbor; they just moved to the elderly apartments, and they are in number twelve."

I could not believe my ears. I thanked the neighbor and got back into the car, heading to Gracie's new home.

I had so many thoughts running through my head, like, *Why did the lady across the street say she had never seen Gracie when she actually lived across the street?* Then I realized how close I came to letting Satan discourage me, how God was in control of every step, and if I had started at each end of the first block, my journey would not have been so long. I was just so thankful I got out of the car and made that last attempt.

When I arrived at apartment twelve, Gracie's daughter opened the door, and I told her who I was and that I had taken care of her mother while she lived with her brother—hoping he hadn't told her that I was a crazy lady that tried to bust his door down. I was in town and was hoping I could see Gracie before I left. She said, "Sure you can; she just went back to her bedroom," and then showed me the way.

There she was, just sitting on the side of her bed. She looked up as I entered, and I told her who I was. She was looking at me strangely but asked me to have a seat by her bed, not taking her eyes off me. I was wondering about her confused look. She then said, "I liked the girl that would come to see me that never saw a machine that pounds and wrenches clothes at the same time." I started laughing and told her that I was that girl. Then it dawned on me: I had colored my hair, and that is what was throwing her off. When I told her that, she said she knew something was different but couldn't figure it out. We then laughed and greeted each other with a big hug. I then asked Gracie if she remembered the last conversation we had about Jesus and whether she'd asked Jesus to forgive her.

"Yes, I do remember," she replied, "and I was hoping I would see you again. I wanted to ask Jesus to save me, but I didn't want to get it wrong."

I said, "Gracie, there is no right way or wrong way. It is believing that Christ died, was buried, and rose again to save you from your sins." She said she did believe it, and right then and there, I held her hand, and she asked Jesus into her heart. She prayed the sweetest prayer of forgiveness, and we both were wiping tears of joy. I told her I would try and be back soon, but if not, I would see her in heaven, and now she was going there too.

Satan should be ashamed, fighting so hard for the life of a precious little lady. But what I realized, and have over and over again many times in my life, was the battle was also between God and me—God telling me to do something and me fighting it because it sounded impossible, completely crazy, or out of the norm for me. As I drove home, I reminisced on it all, asking God to forgive me for doubting Him and rejoicing at Satan's defeat.

TO GOD BE THE GLORY!!!

My prayer is that you know our Sweet Jesus, you are daily in His Holy Bible, and that you don't just read it but believe every word and apply His Word to your life. I pray you are walking and talking with Him. He has work to be done for His glory if you seek His will for you.

> *My sheep hear my voice, and I know them, and they follow me: And I give unto them eternal life; and they shall never perish, neither shall any man pluck them out of my hand. My Father, which gave them to me, is greater than all; and no man is able to pluck them out of my Father's hand. I and my Father are one.*
> —John 10:27–30

Mommy, Please Come Home

Mommy, please come home. Mommy, please come home! Those were the words of a precious little girl crying as I sat across the room from her in a mental ward visiting room.

It was a Sunday afternoon, and I had gone with my friend Karen to see a friend of hers who was in the hospital suffering from a mental breakdown. We went into a large room where all the patients were waiting for their family and friends to visit. That is where I saw the little girl crying. Her mother's head was bent down, trying to calm the girl down. Two older ladies sat by the mother and daughter with sad looks on their faces. I asked Karen's friend Lilly if she knew when the little girl's mother was going to be able to leave. Lilly said if the mother didn't start eating, her doctor was going to begin intravenously feeding her. Her mother had anorexia.

It seemed the mother would see herself in the mirror or through a glass and see herself as larger than she really was. Lilly said the mother made a statement that she wished she was as small as her. That statement really threw me for a loop because Lilly weighed around 300 pounds, while the mother—although I could only see her side profile—was around 100 pounds. I left the hospital feeling pretty sad for that family and confused about how someone could not see that they were skinny instead of fat after looking in a mirror.

Around the dinner table that night, I told my husband and two daughters about the sadness I had encountered at the hospital. I just couldn't get that little girl off my mind and really didn't understand how something was messing that mother's mind up so badly.

I worked for the highway department at the time, and the next day was Monday. I was going to work with my buddy Snuffy. I loved that guy—he was honest, kind, funny, and a true friend. Our job that day was flagging for a man on a backhoe digging out ditches in Greenway, Arkansas. If you know anything about Greenway, it is a jog in the road, population 172, with not much traffic going on around there, so it was going to be a long day. What I do know is it was where God was wanting me to work that day, without a doubt.

So Snuffy was at one end of the road, and I was at the other directing traffic for the backhoe. On days I knew I was going to be flagging, instead of driving a truck, I would carry a small transistor radio in my shirt, so I could listen to Christian radio. I loved the Christian station WCRV out of Collierville, Tennessee, but that morning I forgot to bring it. It was quiet, and I was alone—a perfect place to get alone with God to talk and pray about that child and her mother. I started out asking God how in the world anyone could, in their right mind, not see they were very sick and skinny. I said, "Lord, that is just crazy. All she has to do is open her mouth, put the food in, and chew. I just don't understand how she can stand in front of a mirror and not be able to see that she is skin and bones. Lord, You gave the mother to that little girl, and now I am praying for You to heal that mommy. Father, how can a person get in that kind of shape? What in the world is wrong with her mind? How does this happen? How does it stop? Father, the doctor is going to have nursing start feeding that mother intravenously if You don't intervene."

All of a sudden, I started crying; the thought of that mother without control over her mind and body scared me for myself and my own daughters. How can Satan grab ahold of a mind like that? I asked God to send great and mighty angels to fight the demons that had that poor mother in bondage. She just was not strong enough to fight this battle herself. Still praying, it became clear to me that she was seeing through blinders that Satan had placed over her eyes. I cried out to God to remove those blinders. I told Him she was not strong enough and asked Him to please let her see through God's eyes and restore her sight. Weeping uncontrollably, I stood in the street when all of a sudden, a feeling of peace overflowed me like a load had just been lifted off my shoulders. I stood in awe at the lightness I felt, and then I said, "Lord, I know as well as I'm standing here You healed that mother. I don't even know her name, and I know I will never see her again, but I know You have healed her, and I want to thank You."

Standing in the street, now just crying from the pure joy that was in my heart, was something that I can't explain. It had me so emotional standing there that a passenger in a red truck going by rolled down his window and asked, "Are you all right?"

And I said, "Just go on!"

Finally, it was lunchtime. Snuffy and I were eating lunch in the truck, and all of a sudden, he said, "You sure were doing a lousy job down at the other end flagging."

"I only had one truck all morning," I replied, "and you didn't have anyone, so what are you complaining about?"

We both laughed, and then Snuffy said, "Yeah, your truck stopped when they got to me and said there was something bad wrong with that girl down at the other end; she was crying. But I told them that no, she's all right—she's just been praying." I looked at Snuffy and started crying, telling him about what had just happened. He said he hoped the lady was healed and got back home where she belonged.

When I got home, our family was around the dinner table, and I told them about what had happened. I knew it was hard to believe, but no one could ever tell me that God did not heal that mother and that she was going to be back with her daughter.

For days I was still thanking God for His healing, and then I would have to laugh when I would think about what Snuffy said about knowing I was praying. When I asked him how he knew—I worked on the highway but have never ever known of anyone knowing—he said, "Well, there you were with lifted hands, crying like a baby. What else was I to think?"

A few months later, my daughter Montana and I were standing in the exchange line at Walmart. The line was long, and we had been in it for about thirty minutes. I only had one person in front of me when a lady walked in the doors of the store. One look at her and the words, "Lord, I know I will never see her again, but I know as well as I'm standing here You healed her," came to my mind. You see, I never saw the mother's full face in the hospital that day, so I was shocked that those words were so powerful in my mind. But as I looked, standing beside her was the little girl whose face I would never forget. I could not believe my eyes—I wanted to jump out of line and tell her how the Lord put her on my heart to pray for her. So I said, "Lord, I know this is a divine appointment, but I am next in line, so please keep her here until I return my clothes, and I will go tell her what You did for her." Then I bent down and asked Montana if she remembered the story about the little girl crying for her mother to come home, and she said yes. So I told Montana that they both had just entered the store, and when I returned our clothes, I was going to ask the mother if I could talk to her. I thought we could go back to the toys so she could keep the daughter busy while I told her mother about the Lord putting her on my heart to pray for her.

When we got done with the return, the mother was leaning against a bin in the middle of the aisle. I approached her and told her my name and asked her if she had been in the hospital a few months back, and she said yes. I told her I would like to talk to her and asked if it would be okay if we took our daughters to the toy department while we talked, to which she said yes.

I told her how I was affected by the crying of her daughter that day, which led me to pray for her. I told her how God had put her on my heart, telling her about that day on the highway flagging. I told her that this was a divine appointment and asked her if she knew the Lord Jesus Christ as her personal Lord and Savior. She told me that she did know Christ, and she and her daughter were back in church. She said she was so glad I told her about God putting her on my heart and so thankful I was obedient.

"You see, I was hit with devastating news. My husband, who I adored and thought he adored me, came home and said he wanted a divorce. He literally told me he was leaving me for someone much skinnier than me. Something just snapped in me, and I will tell you, you are right; it was straight from Satan. But one day, when they were going to force-feed me, I looked in the mirror, and it scared me to death seeing how thin I was. And that was the day I turned around and started getting better, and I now know where my strength came from. Thank you for praying for a complete stranger."

I hope someday she reads this book and knows this story is hers. Or it might be yours, or you might be the one who has hurt another for your own lustful desires. Just know nothing gets past God, and He cares for His own, but He is also ready to forgive.

I pray this mother and little girl are living and rejoicing in the goodness of God's love.

> *And in that day shall ye say, Praise the Lord, call upon his name, declare his doings among the people, make mention that his name is exalted.*
> *—Isaiah 12:4*

Lord, Please Help That Lady

There are times when you see a situation and all it seems you can do is pray. That was how I felt on one very hot day leaving Sikeston, Missouri.

I was working for a home health company and drove to Sikeston to see a few clients there. It was very hot outside, and I was headed back to Poplar Bluff, Missouri, to see a few more clients before ending my day. I was driving up a ramp, looking to my left, making sure no traffic was close as I merged out onto the highway. When I merged, I saw straight ahead and to the right of me was a lady walking on the shoulder of the road. She was a large lady, looking to weigh about 300 pounds, with two backpacks on her back, one in her hand, and she was pulling a large suitcase with the other hand. She was headed for a steep climb, and there was nothing I could do to help her. You see, I was in a company car and was not allowed to give anyone a ride.

My heart just dropped, and I cried out, "Lord, please help that lady. There is no way she can make it up that hill in this heat. I don't know how she is going to make it without Your help. Please send someone to pick her up and help her. Please bless that lady, Lord—she needs You! Please bless her in a mighty way."

Soon I was over the hill, and she was out of sight but not out of mind; I could not stop praying for her, worrying about her safety. I had two more clients to see when I got back to Poplar Bluff, and the whole time I was wondering and praying for that lady constantly.

With the drive back to the Bluff from Sikeston and seeing my two clients, it had been at least four hours since I'd seen the lady on the shoulder of the road. I was ready to go home but decided to go to the grocery store before heading that way. As the cashier checked out my items, I saw a large lady with a backpack in her hand come walking toward me, fixing to walk out the door of the store. I thought, *Boy, that is weird seeing another large lady carrying a backpack. At least this lady doesn't have two on her back and pulling a suitcase—or does she?* As the cashier was packing up my groceries, I watched the lady go out the door, and I moved so I could see her. She got behind the shopping carts, where she put on her two backpacks, grabbed her suitcase, and walked out the door.

I was in pure shock, walking back to the checkout line. I said, "God, I asked You to bless that lady, and again You have put her in my presence. I would like to help her if You show me what car she is in." I paid for my groceries and went out the door, but the lady was nowhere in sight. I went up and down the parking lanes, looking at each car, but she was not where I could see her. So I slowly drove away, past the grocery store, heading toward the exit road, and I saw feet sticking out on the pavement by a department store. And there she was—sitting on the pavement, leaning her back against a pillar.

So I pulled up, rolled down my window, and she lifted herself off the ground and came to my passenger window. I asked, "Hello, I was wondering, did I see you leaving Sikeston about four hours ago?"

"Yes, I was there earlier today," she replied.

I told her that I had seen her and was so worried about her in all this heat. I told her that I would have picked her up, but as she could see, I was in a company car, and they would not allow me to do that. I told her that I had prayed for her and asked God to bless her, and then it just so happened that I saw her again in the store just now and felt I needed to help her. I asked her where she was going, and she said Springfield, Missouri. I gave her some money and told her I would be praying for her to have a safe trip and that I believed God was going to protect her all the way.

When I got home, I told my husband, Gary, about the lady, and he said, "Let's go take her to Springfield."

"I don't believe she is there; she may have gotten a room for the night, or she may be on the road, but one thing I believe with all my heart she is in God's hands, and she will make it to Springfield safely."

So many times in my life, I have prayed about a situation and never known the outcome, and then there are other times when God lets me be a part of making that prayer come alive. And then there are times that I feel like I have just been tested, and that might have been an angel. No matter the thought, I am always left with the truth that God hears and answers prayers.

> *And whatsoever ye shall ask in my name, that will I do, that the Father may be glorified in the Son.*
> *—John 14:13*

You Can't Outsmart God

I don't know about you, but I have to know without a shadow of a doubt that God wants me to do a certain thing before I attempt doing it—especially if it has anything to do with teaching or speaking the things of God. The Lord knows this about me, and I have wrestled many times with Him before I do what I think He is asking. I have to know in my heart that it is His will and not mine.

One Sunday morning, as I sat in church, Pastor Steve mentioned a couple wanted to start an addiction recovery program, Reformers Unanimous, in our church on Friday nights. He asked if there would be any members in the church who would be willing to be a part of this program and encouraged those interested to meet with Gus and Erica after church. Pastor Steve had them stand so everyone would know who they were. I instantly knew that I wanted to be a part of this, but there was no way I was going to approach them without praying about it first, even though I knew with all my heart I needed to be a part of this group.

After church, I stood back in the foyer praying and watching to see if anyone was going up to Gus and Erica to give them help and support. I was praying that God would send them good and dedicated workers. The whole time I knew I should have gone to Gus and Erica and let them know that I would love to do what I could to help, but I would not do it. I just would not budge.

Immediately, I started praying for this new program coming to our church. I prayed for each individual who would enter the doors on Friday nights, asking God if He would put four mighty angels at the four corners of our church to fight the demons that were going to try to come in on the backs of each one. I prayed for Gus and Erica, asking God to keep their desire ignited for the lost souls that would be coming for answers to their bondage that seemed impossible to break. I prayed for the workers and the protection of each one's heart to be right with God. I prayed constantly.

A few weeks later, Pastor Steve mentioned again that Reformers Unanimous—which we called RU—was fixing to start, and workers were still needed, reminding those who were interested to go see Gus and Erica after church.

I knew in my heart that I was supposed to help, but I would not go and commit. Again, I stood in the foyer praying and watching for God to send them workers—after all, I had been praying fervently for this program—but I would not go and commit to helping.

On the drive home, I was troubled in my soul for not going and letting them know I was ready to help. I had not even talked to Gary about how I was feeling or what he thought about it. There was a battle going on, so finally, I said, "Lord, if you want me to be a part of RU, then you are going to have to put Erica and me face-to-face." That was it! That was all I said, and the funny thing was, I knew that was not going to happen—or so I thought. You see, I sat on the opposite side of the church than her, and we went out separate doors to leave. In fact, I had never seen her and Gus before the day Pastor Steve had them stand so people would recognize them to volunteer. Yep, I thought we would never meet face-to-face; the odds were against it. It was not that I didn't want to help, but I knew what a great responsibility it was going to be, dealing with people's torn-up lives. I just needed to know it was God who wanted me to be a part of this program and not just my desire.

We were having dinner after church one day, and I went to the church kitchen to get my dish and put it on the serving table. As I was going through the kitchen door, Erica was coming out, and we about knocked each other down. There I stood, literally face-to-face with Erica, and out of my mouth came the words DO YOU STILL NEED WORKERS IN

RU? She replied yes, so I told her I would be glad to help and gave her my name and phone number.

I was so amazed at what God just did that I wanted to laugh and cry. On the way home, I told Gary about my struggle and what God just did and that I was going to help with RU. He thought it would be a great program to be a part of and said he would go with me and do what he could do to help also.

Gary and I were a part of RU for five years until I started taking care of my mother full-time. I will cherish those years and the friendships that I still have to this day. It thrills my soul to run into the ladies that I had in my class, always letting me know that they knew I truly cared for them and prayed for them. God allowed Gary and I to run into a few ladies, on separate occasions this year, who we were able to bless financially because God had blessed us, and they were deeply in need of help. Neither one ever asked for money—they just asked for prayers—but I knew God had put us together, face-to-face, so we could be God's blessing to their prayers.

As for me, I still ask God to show me what His will is for me because I don't want to be out of it, and I don't want to be where I don't belong. One thing I did learn that day as I stood face-to-face meeting with Erica is YOU CAN'T OUTSMART GOD!

My prayer is that you will seek God with all your heart, soul, and mind.

> *The steps of a man are established by the Lord, when he delights in his way.*
> *—Psalm 37:23*

God Owns It All

My husband and I made a move from Corning, Arkansas, to Wappapello, Missouri. Our daughter J'Anna and her family moved into our house in Corning. We had the house for sale even though she was living in it. At the time, it seemed there was a house for sale on every corner, on every street in Corning.

Seven years had passed, and J'Anna was still living in our house, but she'd notified me that they were looking to buy a home across town. I understood completely but was not ready to be a landlord to strangers. I was hoping that our house would have already sold by that time. I had asked the realtor to go down on the price several times in the last seven years because houses were just not selling.

One day J'Anna called and said she thought we said we had gone down on the price, and I told her we had. She said the hometown paper had the price of the house listed, and it was not reduced. So I called the realtor asking why the reduced price was not in the paper. He told me that they talk about it when they show the home. I told him I wanted the reduction put in the paper, but it never happened. I started praying for the house to sell because I didn't want an empty house, nor did I want to rent to strangers.

In the meantime, I also was asking God to show me what He wanted us to give to our church. We were going to have a sacrificial offering at church to kick it off, then ask God what He wanted us to give weekly to the fund to get the building paid off.

I was driving to see my friend Martine Tubb, who I called Marty. I started praying, "Lord, please help me. I feel so overwhelmed because we need to sell our house, but most importantly, we don't have anything to give that would be a sacrifice for the building offering. What do You want, Lord? I feel we have nothing to give, but if You show me, I will give it gladly."

As I pulled into Ms. Marty's parking lot, as clear as anything I have ever heard from God, He said that He wanted my house in Corning. I literally started to chuckle and said, "Lord, if You can sell that house, You can have it. There is just one thing I ask. There's a couple in our church who have surrendered to the mission field and are on the road, getting support from other churches. I would like to give them 10 percent of the sale on the house to help with their traveling expenses. I would like to give my parents 10 percent since they are going through a hard time right now, and the money would help them out a lot. And if You will allow me to help my brother out with a 10 percent gift, I know he has those little triplets to raise, and he could use the help. If this is not pleasing to You, please let me know as only You can. I will give the rest to the church building fund."

When I went in to see Ms. Marty, she asked what took me so long to get out of my car. I told her that I was talking to God and just gave Him our house in Corning. She started laughing, and I found myself laughing with her. I started telling her about what had just happened and that I knew that God wanted the money from the house that had been for sale for seven years. I knew it sounded crazy, but I knew as well as I was standing there that God was going to get that house sold.

When I got home, Gary and I got ready and went to Wednesday night services and then to our workout afterward. While we were walking on the treadmills, I realized I had not told Gary that I had given our house to the church building fund. So I got off my treadmill and walked up to Gary and said, "Babe, will you get off the treadmill for a minute so I can tell you what I did today?"

While still walking, he said to go ahead and tell him; he was listening.

I said, "No, you really need to get off. It is pretty serious, and I don't want you walking when I tell you."

So he got off the treadmill, and I proceeded to tell him how I gave our house to God today, and it was going to go to the building fund.

"What did you do that for, and where are we going to live?" he asked.

"Oh, not our house in Wappapello. I'm talking about the house in Corning."

With a laugh, he said, "Well, if He can sell it, He can have it."

The very next day, I again was on my way to Ms. Marty's house, and as soon as I pulled into her parking lot, my phone rang. It was J'Anna. She was talking when all of a sudden, she said, "Mom, I need to go. Sandra just pulled up in the drive."

I asked if it was neighborhood Sandra, meaning a girl who grew up in our neighborhood. She said yes and said she would call me back later.

As soon as she hung up, the sweet voice of God said, "Sandra is going to buy your house." I was so sure of His voice that I went inside Ms. Marty's house and said, "Guess what? My house is being sold right now. God sold my house in one day!" I told her what just happened, and she got so tickled I didn't think she was ever going to stop laughing. She said if she didn't love me so much, she would call me crazy.

It was not long before my phone rang again—it was J'Anna. With excitement, she said, "Mother, Sandra wants to buy your house!"

Out loud, I said, "What?! Sandra wants to buy my house?" Oh, I will never forget the expression on Marty's face when she heard those words. I can tell you her smile turned into a look of disbelief—it was priceless. J'Anna continued to tell me that the bank told Sandra how much they would give her to buy a home, so Sandra went and got the newspaper to view the home listings.

"And, Mother, guess what?" J'Anna said, "After all this time, this was the first time the realtor put the reduction price in the paper, and it was the amount the bank said they would lend her, so she drove right over here to let us know she wanted to buy your house."

I was still at Marty's house, and I started telling J'Anna what happened the day before and how quickly God answered my prayers, and we looked forward to fulfilling our commitment to Him.

As far as Ms. Marty, it was no mistake that she happened to be a part of those two days. It changed a lot of things in her life that day. Many times, she would say, "I still can't get over how you gave your house to the Lord, and you knew He wanted it without a shadow of a doubt. I want to know Him more." She got even closer to God by studying His Word and praying. And we had great times praising the Lord together until He took her home.

I love my Gary. I know many are saying I should have talked to Gary before giving our house away. But you know, I have to do what God tells me to do, and He will prepare the way and hearts of all involved. I truly thank God for a husband who knows it is all God's anyway and that when God speaks, we should obey. We just want God to have His way for His glory.

I am thankful everything went smoothly, and all who I wanted to receive money were given that gift.

Thank You again, Father, for those wonderful two days that were as exciting as any I have ever known. You, Lord, are truly an awesome God! Thank You for Your direction in our lives. Please bless and encourage the reader of this story to seek You and give it all to You. Amen.

Trust in the Lord with all thine heart; and lean not unto thine own understanding. In all thy ways acknowledge him, and he shall direct thy paths.
Proverbs 3:5–6

God Knows Our Every Need

Have you ever been in need of a car but did not have the available funds to purchase one? That is where Gary and I have been several times in our life, but God never failed us one time.

Gary was walking to work, which he always did, and I drove the car. But now we had our oldest daughter, J'Anna, expecting her first child, living with us at the time. She was working but didn't have a car.

I sat down at the kitchen table and asked God to show us what we could afford. I wrote down all our bills and subtracted that total from our income. It was plain to see we could not afford even $100 a month. The thought came to my mind that if I didn't tithe, we could afford a car, but that was the only place I could cut back on. But there was NO WAY I was going to do that, not after our Pastor Steve preached on tithing. I knew that I did not want to rob God.

So it was settled. Gary would continue to walk to work, and J'Anna and I would have to share the car we had. It was very plain to see we would not be getting a car anytime soon—or so I thought. Gary had other plans, and he told me to get ready to go look at cars in the morning.

"Gary, we cannot afford a car," I replied. "In fact, I am thinking of getting a bicycle and riding it to work."

He said we could just go look. Boy, did the prayers start flowing then. In fact, I had just accepted that we didn't have the money for a car and that, in time, we would be able to buy one, but not right now.

The next day we drove out of town to a dealership, and Gary told the car salesman that we needed a car for $100 a month. I thought, *Where in the world was he going to get the money to make that kind of payment?* I was truly scared to death. I began to think about the extra money for insurance. I cried out in my mind, "Father, help us! I don't know what to do!"

The salesman said, "Sure, I have five Geo Prizms in the gated area behind the dealership. Let's go back there so you can give them all a test drive. Let me know your choice, and I will sell any one of them to you for $100 a month."

The salesmen gave us the keys to all five cars, and we got into car number one. We had to call the gentleman back because the car would not start, but they gave it a boost and off we went. I could tell there was something wrong with the brakes right from the start. I asked Gary if he could tell there was a problem, and he said yes. We went back to car number two. The man had to come out and give that car a boost also, then off we went. You could tell that the car had some major problems even before we got out of the gate. I told Gary that we didn't need to go too far because the car was a piece of junk.

I was ready to go home. I saw that these cars were pure junk. I was praying every step of the way. We were about to get into car three, but when we opened the doors, we had to quickly shut them. That car smelled like a huge cat litter box; it was horrible. Lord, help us! So we moved on to Geo Prizm number four. Same story—the salesman had to come give the car a jump start, and it was a rattletrap.

By now, I was really feeling sorry for Gary. When we got in Geo number five, it also had to be given a boost, but he said, "Well, this is the best out of the five, so I think we need to go ahead and buy it."

Tears started flowing. I knew he just wanted to provide us a car that was deeply needed, but it didn't stop the fact that we did not have any extra money to purchase it. He pulled up to the front of the dealership, fixing to buy the car, when I said, "Gary, if you want that car, then you need to get a second job to pay for it because it is not in our budget. You will have to go in there by yourself and put it in your name because I will not have anything to do with it. I showed God our budget, and He knows we cannot afford a car, and I am not going to pretend we can." The whole time I was crying because the situation we were in really hurt, and I knew it was hurting my Gary most of all. He never said a word. He just pulled out of the drive, and we went home.

A few days later, I was driving the highway truck back to town to the highway department office, where I was working at the time. I happened to notice a red Geo Prizm coming down the road, and as it approached, I saw the driver's hand go up, and he was waving. The person that was waving happened to be my husband. Gary had a big smile on his face, and I felt my face drop in shock. I wondered, *What in the world has he done?* It was the end of the day, and I was back at the office waiting with the other workers for the clock to strike five so we could leave. I looked out the window and saw Gary pull into the parking lot in that red Geo Prizm.

The clock struck five, and out of the building I walked straight to my smiling husband while my coworkers were hollering, "Hey, Jeanie, did you get a new car?" I just smiled and kept walking.

When I reached Gary, he gave me a hug and said, "Babe, this afternoon, my parents came by and took me to lunch. After we ate, they drove me by our house, and there was this car sitting in our drive. They said that they knew we could probably use another car, and they wanted to give the Geo to us. They said they had done so much for my brother, so they wanted to do something for me."

No one knew we were in need of a car but me, Gary, and God. I was just amazed at how close we came to buying a car we could not afford. The very kind of car we were looking at was right in front of me—only this one didn't need to be boosted, the brakes were good, it didn't smell like a litter box, and it didn't cost us a dime. Yep, no one knew but God.

The lesson is God hears our prayers, and God is faithful to supply our needs, but we also need to be faithful to Him. We show our faith in giving, trusting, and obeying. It is a humbling place to be when you know God is your only hope. I can tell you it gets more humbling when you know you are nothing without Him.

Father, you are so kind and patient. Forgive us when we try to outdo You or when we try to want more than You want us to have. Thank You for the wonderful blessings You so graciously bestow upon us, for we are so undeserving. But You call us blessed. Most certainly, I want to thank You for my Gary, for he is one of the finest and rarest gifts You have given me. Without him and his patience, we may not see You as clearly as we need to. Amen.

> *My brethren, count it all joy when ye fall into divers temptations; Knowing this, that the trying of your faith worketh patience. But let patience have her perfect work, that ye may be perfect and entire, wanting nothing.*
> *If any of you lack wisdom, let him ask of God, that giveth to all men liberally, and upbraideth not; and it shall be given him. But let him ask in faith, nothing wavering. For he that wavereth is like a wave of the sea driven with the wind and tossed. For let not that man think that he shall receive any thing of the Lord. A double minded man is unstable in all his ways.*
> *—James 1:2–8*

OH LORD, THIS FAMILY NEEDS YOU

I worked as a home health aide for over twenty-three years. I loved my job, and I am so thankful for each and every person that God brought into my life. Although my job was to care for those who needed help, I knew my real job was to make sure my clients knew the Lord as their Savior. You could say the company I worked for paid me, but I worked for the Lord, and what a joy that was. I can truthfully say I looked so forward to going to work each and every day.

Then came the day I really thought I had met my match, and this would be the one I would let Satan have. I just didn't feel the fight within me, and the man I had as a client was just mean. Every other word out of his mouth was saying God's name in vain. I am serious—every other breath. He would spew his filth if you touched him, when you turned him, even if you looked at him, and he tried to bite me on several occasions. But the saddest part was his little children heard every word. I was sick to my stomach at the end of the visit.

When I left after the first visit, I got in my car and said, "Lord, this family needs you, but I cannot take care of this man. I cannot take him cursing Your name." Then I just broke into tears. I could not believe I stayed the whole time listening to him curse my Lord. Oh, how I wanted to stick that bar of soap in his mouth.

A few days later, it was time to make another visit, but this time he had been moved to a nursing home, and for that, I was thankful. I was thinking things might be a little better—if not for me, then at least for those sweet children. I walked into his room, and he gave me a mean look. I stood beside his bed and told him my name and that I was there to give him his bath if he didn't mind. All he would do was give me a dirty look. So I started getting his bath pans ready, and the cursing of God's name began over and over again. It took me thirty minutes to shave him while he tried to bite me and snarled the whole time. I had to roll him onto his side, but he would fight me, so I stepped out into the hall to get an aide to help. When I asked the aide to help me, you could see the look of dread on her face, but she came anyway. As soon as I got done and laid him on his back again, the aide couldn't get out of the room quick enough. And I had made up my mind: I WAS NOT EVER GOING TO TAKE CARE OF HIM AGAIN!

I got everything cleaned up after his bath and then sat in a chair right next to his bed to do my charting. I was writing down how he acted so that it would be on record when I told the agency I was never going back to care for this man. I looked up, and he was staring at me and called me an awful name. That is when I rose up from my chair, pointed my finger in his face, and lit into him with a fiery rage of anger! I started crying because I was boiling mad. I knew I was going to give him a piece of my mind before I left his room, and I was never coming back. I said, "You know what, mister? You are at a crossroads, and it is going to lead you to heaven or hell. You are fixing to spend eternity in one of those places, and I am pretty sure it is going to be in hell. Yes, sir, and there is no turning back. And my God, who you so boldly are cursing, is the very God who could save you. His name is Jesus, and He suffered and died so that you can have eternal life with Him in heaven. He died on a cruel cross, not for you to cry out His name to curse Him, but to cry out to save a wicked man like you. You need to be asking Jesus to forgive you of your cussing and every other bad thing you have done and to come into your heart and live—what is left of it—because you, my son, have a very short time left in this world. Satan and his hell are waiting on you; you can be sure of it! Satan is fighting for your soul, and it looks like he is winning. But I am telling you right now, I WILL NOT BE BACK to listen to you curse my Lord and Savior's name again."

The whole time I was in a rage of anger, and he never took his eyes off me. Then he started crying, but I was not done with him. I had more to say before I left and never came back. So I continued my rant when all of a sudden, God got ahold of me to be kinder and show love as I spoke. Believe me when I say I have never been that mad in my life.

So now we were both crying, but with a softer voice, I said, "Buddy, you are at a crossroads, and that God you love to cuss says He loves you, He died for you, and will take away your sins, along with that cursing. Jesus wants to give you a new life and a home in heaven with Him when you die if you would only ask Him to forgive you and to take control of your life by letting Jesus into your life."

We were crying like babies, my tears first flowing from anger but now flowing in sympathy for this lost and dying man. His tears might have been out of fear at first, but his weeping was showing brokenness. So I said, "I am going to lay my hand on your chest and pray for you. Then I am going to say a prayer that you can pray with me and ask God to save your soul and change your life. Now you can pray that prayer if you want Christ to save you, or you can ignore it all. But I will tell you this: I will come back one more time, but if you curse me even one time, I will walk out the door immediately and never return."

I prayed for him and then laid my hand on his chest and said if he would like to repeat after me, he could repeat out loud or to himself; the choice was his. I prayed, "God, please forgive me. I am a sinner who is in need of Your Saving Grace. I believe You suffered and died for my sins, and I want to thank You for that sacrifice, so I don't have to pay that price myself. I believe You died and rose again from the grave, and You won the victory over death, the grave, and my sins so that I can live in Your victory and in Your love and presence. I am asking You to save my soul, to come into my life, and to make me like You. Show me what I need to change so others can see You in me. Thank You, Lord Jesus, for saving my soul and giving me a home in heaven to spend the rest of my life with You. Amen."

He never opened his eyes when I finished. So I sat down by his bed and completed my charting. As I rose out of the chair to leave, he opened his eyes and said, "Thank you, pretty lady." I smiled and said I would see him Wednesday.

I got out to my car and cried out to God, asking what in the world just happened. I asked God to forgive me for hollering at that poor man. I bet he thought I was a crazy lady shouting fire and brimstone at him. And then I prayed that he really did understand what I was saying to him through the crying and yelling and that he did ask Christ into his life.

When I returned on Wednesday, I peeked around the door and saw he was watching TV. He turned his head toward the door and smiled really big when he saw me. I said, "Do I need to throw my hat in the door first?" He laughed and asked me to come on in. I did everything I needed for him, and he never once said or did anything out of the way. In fact, everyone who came down the hall of the nursing home would stop at the door and ask if I noticed how calm and nice he was. I would look at him and say, "Did you tell them I put the wrath of God in you?" He would get so tickled. The change in him was remarkable. He and I had the best time joking and laughing. I would bring my book by The Pacific Garden Rescue Mission and read to him about other lives that were changed by the love of Jesus. I would read the Bible to him, and I would watch TV with him so he could have a conversation and know that I was there for him.

A few weeks went by, and an aide that had just come back to work from vacation came walking through his room shouting vulgarity. She walked over to the other side of his bed and said, "How are you doing, you old . . ." It was horrible what was coming out of her mouth. There he lay with his eyes bulging out of his head, looking up at the ceiling.

I said, "I don't know who you think you are, but don't you ever come back into this room and say anything but kindness to this man. Using profanity? Who do you think you are talking to a patient like that?"

She said she was just beating him to the punch, as he called her dirty names all the time. His eyes were fixed on the ceiling, and his face was red as a beet. He was not saying a word, and he wouldn't look at either one of us. I just bet he wished the Lord would have taken him home in an instant.

So I then asked the aide the last time he had called her a dirty name. She said she didn't know, but it was before she left for vacation two weeks ago. I said, "Exactly. So he doesn't say those words anymore." Looking at him, I said, "DO YOU?" He shook his head no. I said, "He will not be calling you names or cursing, and you should never curse anyone in a nursing home, so don't ever do that again in this room, or I will report you."

The aide left the room, and I told him to look at me. I said, "If I ever hear of you cursing anyone ever again, I am going to cut your tongue out. Do you understand me?" He looked at me and shook his head yes, and then we both started laughing.

I always left him as my last client of the day, so I could spend time getting to know him and sharing the greatness of God. He never again said a bad word. Everyone commented on how he was a changed man, and he would smile his biggest smile. We became great friends, forever friends, and then God took him home to spend eternity with Him. Now he is my eternity friend.

Thank You, Lord Jesus, for knowing our personalities so well. You know just what kind of person can lead another to You. Help us to be ready daily to plant seeds into the lives around us and thank You for the ones You allow us to see come full bloom. May we be ready to be used by You. Fill us with Your holy presence to complete the task You set before us. Amen.

> *And grieve not the holy Spirit of God, whereby ye are sealed unto the day of redemption. Let all bitterness, and wrath, and anger, and clamour, and evil speaking, be put away from you, with all malice: And be ye kind one to another, tenderhearted, forgiving one another, even as God for Christ's sake hath forgiven you.*
> *—Ephesians 4:30–32*

WHEREVER HE LEADS, I'LL GO

You know when God is calling you to do something, but you just come up with a thousand excuses not to do it?

For some time, God was calling me to go to church and find a room to pray for our pastor and the congregation during the service. That thought came to my mind every Sunday morning as I was getting ready, but I came up with every excuse not to. The main excuse was I wanted to be fed. I did not want to miss what God put on our pastor's heart. You know, many go to church willingly but want to get out by noon. I truly would not care if Pastor Steve preached two hours longer; I enjoyed every word. I can truly say I don't think I have ever left a service that I wasn't changed in some way or that I needed to change something in my life. I just did not want to give that up—not just the preaching but the singing as well. I needed them both to get me through the week. Still, the thought came to me every Sunday while getting ready, and I will admit I ignored it.

The men in our Sunday school class were leaving ten minutes early to pray before services, and I thought that would be a good time for me to find a place to pray for ten minutes as well. I just came up with one excuse after another until one morning, the calling to pray was overwhelming.

I said, "Okay, Lord, if this is really what You want me to do, then You have to prove it to me loud and clear. Just show me, and I will do it. But I need to know this is of You." As soon as I opened my bathroom door, a preacher on our TV asked in a loud voice: "What are you doing in your church to glorify God?" The words hit me like a ton of bricks. I shut my bathroom door, sat on my vanity chair, and said, "I will start today, Lord.

I will leave after the singing. I am looking forward to our time together. Please forgive me for stalling on this."

It took me a little time to find the perfect room to pray in. I wanted to be close to the auditorium, so I would know when the services were ending because I don't wear a watch, and I didn't want my husband waiting on me after church. The rooms that were close to the auditorium were used at the end of the services to deal with people who came forward for salvation. So I finally went upstairs to a classroom that had a clock. And that was where I started praying for our pastor, the word that God had put on his heart, the congregation, the Reformer Addiction program, our school, and anything else God put on my heart to pray for.

Week after week, for months, I went to that classroom and prayed. Not only did I pray, but I wrote my prayers down; I find comfort in writing my prayers down so I can go back and read them and thank God for answering them. I would ask Gary what Pastor Steve talked about on the way home after the morning service, and so many times, I would read to him what I was praying about, and it would match the sermon.

One time in particular, I was asking the Lord if He still wanted me to continue going to my prayer room. I guess I was feeling sorry for myself. It had been around six months, and I thought I had prayed for everything over and over. Then, as ashamed as I am to admit it, God put on my heart that I literally hadn't prayed for children's church. A feeling came over me that brought me to tears. How in the world did I forget to pray for them? I prayed many times for the children but never once for the children's church or the dedicated workers.

I started writing and crying, asking God to forgive me. How in the world did I forget the future of our church being taught by dedicated members? So I prayed the whole time for the workers, the precious children, their families, and for every one of those children to receive His Word clearly and ask Christ into their hearts. I was so broken. As I prayed, I realized how many areas of prayer were associated with children's church.

In the evening services that night, Pastor Steve mentioned that they had a praise report in the morning services. He said there were six children saved in the children's church that morning.

What a beautiful time of rejoicing I had in my heart. I thanked God for those dedicated church members who served the Lord through the giving of their talent and teaching those sweet children about Jesus. I thanked God for working through His Word into the lives of those children and giving them the wisdom to answer His knocking on their hearts' door. I also thanked God that He hears our prayers and speaks to us in vivid ways. Then I personally thanked Him for knowing me better than I knew myself, thanking Him for how He reaches me and teaches me. So in my heart, I knew it was His will for me to continue to pray in my prayer room. Not long after that day, I was not able to attend church at all because I was caring for my mother, and it had gotten to the point where I could not leave her alone anymore. I missed my classroom prayer room but never stopped praying.

If this story says anything, I hope it speaks to you just how important it is to pray for your pastor and all the programs going on in your church. I pray you get excited about praying, for it is the greatest source of power to talk to God and experience His answers. What a beautiful gift He has given us!

Thank You, Lord, for the power in Your Word and prayer—all to get to know You better. Amen.

> *Jesus said, "Let the little children come to me,*
> *and do not hinder them, for the kingdom*
> *of heaven belongs to such as these."*
> *—Matthew 19:14*

OH, TO KNOW YOUR VOICE

I went to church all my life but never really understood the power of prayer or how to hear God's voice. All I knew when I turned my life over to Christ was I wanted to know Him personally and recognize His voice.

One of my first encounters with the Holy Spirit's voice occurred while I was driving down a dark road. I had asked my father if I could borrow his El Camino to pick Gary up at a bus station. This was not a car my dad liked to let anyone drive—it was like his own private ride. But he said that I could, so I took off with my little girls to pick up Gary.

We drove to a nearby town, picked Gary up, and headed home. Gary was talking, telling me about his week, and I was driving down a dark country road. All of a sudden, a thought came to my mind: "Be careful—that truck is going to run you off the road." Over and over, that thought came to my mind.

Now, there was barely any traffic, but soon I saw approaching lights. I didn't know if it was a truck or a car until it got closer, and I clearly saw it was a truck. I started slowing down as Gary was talking. I was praying, "Lord, there is a truck ahead. Please protect us, and please don't let me wreck Dad's truck. Please protect us!" I lifted my foot off the gas and started getting ready to hit the side ditch when, all of a sudden, the approaching truck started into my lane. I smoothly rode the El Camino into the ditch until the truck passed. I got us back up on the road and then pulled over to make sure everyone was okay. I was a little shaken up and about to cry, but everyone was fine.

Gary looked at me then with wonder and said, "You acted like you knew that was going to happen."

"I did," I said.

No, I did not tell my dad that I rode a ditch in his truck, but I did tell God how thankful I was that He spoke to me and provided a shield of protection. That still, small voice—what a blessing it is!

My sheep hear my voice and follow me.
—John 10:27

LORD, I CAN'T DO THIS

Just another Sunday morning, my family and I were walking out the door to go to church when the weirdest thought came to my mind: *Stop by Francis's house and ask to use her bathroom.* The problem with that thought was I did not know Francis. Oh, I knew of her and was even praying for her but never talked to her.

Francis was an umpire for our girls' softball games, and she was a waitress at the Stateline Restaurant outside Corning, Arkansas. That is all I knew about Francis, except for the prayer request my friend Karen had asked me to pray. Karen told me Francis had had a heart attack, wrecked her car, and was not able to work. She had moved into a trailer—across from the tourist information center at the Arkansas state line—that a friend let her stay in and would pay her utilities. She had no money and none coming in because she did not qualify for social security at that time due to her age. Francis was literally hanging by the thread of her teeth. When Karen told me all that had happened to Francis, my heart broke, so I started praying for her. But I was not prepared for what God was asking me to do.

We were getting close to the state line, and the thought would not leave my head, so I said, "Gary, when we get to the state line rest area, would you pull in across the street from it at the trailer? Francis lives there, and I am going to use her restroom." He asked me why I was going to her trailer when the rest area was right across the street. I said, "I don't know, but will you do it anyway?" Gary said we would be late for church, but I told him I wouldn't stay long. We sat in silence, and I asked God if He was really speaking to me to do this. I believed He was, but I truly didn't understand why. It all seemed so crazy to me, but I knew in my heart it was what I needed to do.

Standing on her porch, not really understanding why, I knocked on her door. She opened it and looked a little surprised and confused, so I said, "Hello, Francis, I'm Jeanie Selby." She said she knew who I was, so I said, "We are on our way to church, and I was wondering if I could use your restroom."

She said yes and that it was the first door on the left, past the kitchen. As I walked into the kitchen, I saw an open Bible on her table with a cup of coffee beside it. I went into the bathroom, and a feeling of fear overwhelmed me. I was literally looking for a window to climb out of. *I mean, how would that be any crazier than what I am doing now?* I cried out, "LORD, WHAT AM I DOING HERE?" I thought I had surely made a big mistake in hearing God when I asked, "God, please tell me why I am here."

I was ready to go out the door and just thank Francis for letting me use her restroom, chalking this up as a big mistake. But as I was washing my hands, in front of me was a shelf that had five bottles of empty medicine. I looked closer and could see they were two weeks overdue from being filled, and those pills were needed for her heart and health. "This is it, isn't it, Lord? She does not have the money to fill these meds, so you want us to fill them." Fear turned to joy. I walked out the door, and there she stood in the kitchen, still looking a little confused.

"Francis, I wasn't sure why I was to use your bathroom instead of going across the street. Now, please know that I am not a nosey person, but I saw that you have five empty bottles that are past due from being refilled. If you let me, I know that God wants me to get them filled for you."

"I can't let you do that," she responded. "I don't even know you."

"You said you knew who I was when I introduced myself."

"You don't understand. There is no way I could pay you back. You see, I have this roof over my head because a friend has graciously given me a place to live. I have no home. I have no job. I have no insurance. In fact, if I eat today, it will be because God provides it. And I can truthfully say there has not been one day that someone has not brought me a meal."

"Then will you believe me when I tell you that I know God sent me here to fill your medicine? Will you please let me do that for you? Francis, our friend Karen has been telling me about your struggles, and I have been praying for you, so there is no doubt in my mind that God sent me here to fill those meds if you will let me."

Francis went and got the bottles for me and put them in a sack. As she handed them to me, she said, "I hate doing this. I don't think you know how expensive they are going to be."

"My God owns cattle on a thousand hills," I said and told her I would be back in the morning with her pills filled.

This is why prayer is so important. You never know—God might use you to complete or be a part of the success of that prayer. It is a beautiful thing, to say the least. Francis became our lifelong friend, and we watched God give her disability, so she finally had an income. He provided her an apartment where she had great neighbors and a free car and literally gave her life back for many years after. We were better just knowing her, and she became family to us until the Lord called her home. Now we just smile at the thought of seeing her again some sweet day.

Father, thank You for the friend we had in Francis, but most of all for the Friend we have in You. Amen.

> *Shew me thy ways, O Lord; teach me thy paths. Lead me in thy truth, and teach me: for thou art the God of my salvation; on thee do I wait all the day.*
> —Psalm 25: 4–5

GOD, YOU ARE AMAZING

I just want to say, before I start this story: never stop praying for those God has put on your heart to pray for. And if anyone has asked you to pray, do it until the answer comes.

I was standing in the foyer at church when a sweet little lady named Marietta came up to me, took me aside, and said, "I was wondering if you would pray for a nephew of mine."

"Of course I will," I answered. "What is his name, and what is he needing prayer for?"

"His name is Chris," Marietta said, "and he wants out of the homosexual lifestyle. He lives in Florida and works as a schoolteacher. He has been in the homosexual lifestyle since college, he is in his fifties now, and he really needs prayer."

I told her I would be praying for Chris.

Now, I can tell you that the request already felt burdensome. For one, I needed to ask God to help me to pray for this man who lived hundreds of miles away. I mean, he needed to stay in my heart every day if possible. Then I started thinking of how long he had been in that lifestyle. I was sure most of his friends were living the same way, so he needed new friends. He needed a church to go to that had godly workers to help him and not shun him. I also had to ask God to prepare me, as always, to pray with a clean heart. I knew that this was a great desire in Marietta's heart for Chris to be able to turn his life over in complete surrender to the Lord. My job was to pray because I said I would.

I found myself feeling so burdened by Chris; I was constantly praying for him, asking God to help him to withstand the power of Satan in his life. I prayed for God to lead him to a Bible-believing church that would take the time to counsel him in love and understanding. There were times that a song would be on a Christian radio station, and I would have to pull over driving and just cry out the words of the song to the Lord for Chris. I would send him cards of encouragement and a song that I hoped would turn his heart toward Jesus.

I guess I had been praying for Chris for almost a year when the strangest thing happened. I was working in home health and had a client in a nursing home in Campbell, Missouri. The little lady I was going to be taking care of had Alzheimer's. The nurse told me I would never get her in the shower. The nurse said I would not be able to give her a bed bath either. If I was lucky, I might be able to give her a sponge bath, but I should watch her hands because she just might hit me.

Into the client's room I went, but not without praying and asking God to calm her spirit so I could give her a bath. As I entered the room, there was a lady in the first bed who welcomed me into the room. When I told her I was there to give her roommate a bath, she laughed and told me good luck with that. My client was sitting in her wheelchair, so I started talking to her, letting her know what I was there to do. Knowing she probably didn't understand a word I said, I started getting her clothes and water ready. I noticed right off the bat that she was in need of head washing, so I started wrapping a towel around her head. She started screaming and hitting me, so I started singing "Jesus Loves Me" and hugging her. She just melted, and although I had to stop all through the bath to sing and hug her, I got the job completed.

The lady in the other bed, Betty Jo, was amazed that I was getting anything done at all. She told me a little about herself as I cared for my client. It seemed that my client liked the conversation that was going on around her. It also seemed to calm her. Just the name of Jesus seemed to calm her spirit.

As I was getting ready to leave the room, Betty Jo said, "I wish I had a warm washcloth for my face and hands." I told her I would be glad to wash her face and hands and leave the washcloth on the rail of her bed so she could reach it. That was just a special thing I did for her each and every visit, and it was my way of showing her the love of Jesus and letting her know that, although she was not my client, she was just as special to me.

I so enjoyed my visits with Betty Jo as I was bathing my client. She would talk about her life and how she wished she could change it all and start life over with her boys. She told me she was not a good mother. She'd been married several times, and it was a life of fighting and hatred that her boys had to live in—along with her intake of pills that seemed to stop the pain she was in. As she told her stories, I would tell her about the love of Jesus. She said she knew God's love now, but it didn't change the fact that her sons had to live with those awful memories. It was those memories that made her heart break. I would pray for her every day before I would leave.

One day as I was leaving, she said, "I sure hope my sister Marietta comes and sees me today." I asked her if Marietta went to church at Westwood in Poplar Bluff, and she said yes. I told her that I went to the same church, that Marietta was in my Sunday school class, and to tell her I said hello.

I talked with Betty Jo for about three months as I cared for my client, who was surprisingly quiet during our conversations. I attributed this to the Lord's intervention—especially when I was soon to realize what was really going on.

As I was getting ready to go one day, I was washing Betty Jo's face and hands when she asked me if I would do her a favor. She asked me to pray for her son. I said I sure would love to and asked her son's name. She said it was Chris. All of a sudden, Marietta came to my mind, and I remembered Betty Jo saying they were sisters, so I asked her if Chris lived in Florida, and she said yes. You could have knocked me over with a feather. I told her that I had been praying for her son and I would continue, but I did not tell her what I had been praying for.

I got in my car to leave and just started crying out loud, "LORD,

YOU PUT ME IN FRONT OF CHRIS'S MOM?" I was in total shock. I thought, *What if I had never given her a washcloth or washed her face?* She was not my client, and I was not supposed to have anything to do with anyone but my client. I cannot pass up a person in need because I may be in that same shape or position someday. Her hands were crippled, and it was so hard for her to do anything with them. If I hadn't shown her compassion, she might not have felt comfortable sharing her life with me.

Then I thought about how my client was so compliant with everything I did for her; even Betty Jo and the nurses could not believe how calm she was. Without a doubt, that was God calming her so Betty Jo and I could talk. The thought of God putting us together was just blowing me away. My tears just would not stop flowing because I now had a greater understanding of Chris's life. The pain of his life grew greater inside me, my prayers grew more detailed, and my heart became more broken. I cannot remember when I was so burdened.

Over a year had passed, and Marietta called and asked me what I was doing on Saturday, and I told her I had no plans. She told me there was someone who wanted to meet me. I said fine and asked who it was, and she said it was Chris. I was so excited to finally get to put a face on the soul I had been praying for. She told me he wanted to see the three ladies that he knew were praying for him through his journey to God.

I hung up talking to Marietta and just started praising the Lord. God showed me over and over by putting Chris on my heart constantly that he was mine to pray for, and then God put his mother in my life, which was a mind-blower for me. The one thing I didn't understand was when Betty Jo passed away, I was in Oklahoma visiting my sister, so I never got to meet Chris when he came for her funeral. But now I was going to be able to finally meet him, and I was beyond excited.

There he was—a face to my prayers. We hugged like we had known each other our whole lives. We sat down at the kitchen table, and Chris started telling me about going to college and getting involved with a man.

He told how he remembered his Aunt Marietta being boldly against it but also knew she prayed for him. He remembered, as a kid growing up, that you always said the blessing at mealtime and had Bible study in the evening at Marietta's house. Then he started talking about his mother and how hard she was on him and his brother. "That's it, Lord, this moment right now—this is the reason You put Betty Jo and me together, to tell Chris how sorry she was and how she wished she would have raised them better." So that is what I did.

I told him how God put me in a room with his mother for about six months, three times a week. I told him how much she loved him and his brother and wished she had done things differently. I told him about the day she had asked me to pray for him, and then I realized God had me listening to her burdens while I cared for my client because God knew Chris needed to know that she was sorry so healing could come into his life. Not until she asked me to pray for him did I know God had put us together, and she was his mother.

Now, how beautiful is that? I say very beautiful. The love of God is so spectacular. He knew the heart of Betty Jo for her sons, and He knew the heart of Aunt Marietta for her nephew. He knew the heart of another aunt in Arkansas who faithfully prayed for him. God knew my heart for a complete stranger, and God knew the heart of Chris and wanted to help him to get out of the homosexual lifestyle.

It has been at least five years since this all happened. I talked to Chris a couple of weeks ago, and he has been praying for God to send him a godly wife and thought he might have found her. I will be going to Florida in a few weeks and plan on seeing him again.

I hope if you have a loved one in a lifestyle that is not pleasing to God, and it is literally ripping your heart out, please take it to God in prayer. Love the person but not the sin. Chris turned to his Aunt Marietta and his aunt in Arkansas in the time of his despair because he knew they loved him and would not lie to him about his sin. Although they made him angry when he was sinning, they would not fall into the lie of deception.

They were the ones he cried out to in his despair because he saw the solid rock of truth in them. And that is what he needed—solid truth—to get out of something that he said he always knew was wrong. Be that truth, never stop praying, and never stop believing that God hears and answers those prayers.

The answer may not come in the morning—we prayed many years for Chris. Though the answer did not come immediately, we never stopped praying. Satan has complete control only if we stop praying. I know Chris had to allow Christ to move in his life, but it is by our prayers that God can destroy Satan's plan for our loved ones' lives. When you feel helpless, remember: Prayer is almighty power; it is you admitting the power you don't have to change things and giving it to the only One who can.

Father God, if the one reading this story finds themselves in despair over a loved one in a horrible sin, please give them wisdom. Father, without Your wisdom and truth, they cannot be that strong foundation of strength that their loved one will need when they seek to rise out of the darkness. Father, please do not let them compromise Your truth for Satan's lie, but let Your love radiate compassion and kindness that will bring hope and light to the one they are so desperately praying for. Bring their loved one out of the darkness, even today, Lord—even today. In the precious and powerful name of Jesus, I pray, Amen.

> *And be renewed in the spirit of your mind; And that ye put on the new man, which after God is created in righteousness and true holiness.*
> *—Ephesians 4:23–24*

Christopher's verse:

> *And he said to them all, If any man will come after me, let him deny himself, and take up his cross daily, and follow me.*
> *—Luke 9:23*

Aunt Marietta's verse:

> *Trust in the L*ORD *with all thine heart; and lean not unto thine own understanding. In all thy ways acknowledge him, and he shall direct thy paths.*
> *—Proverb 3:5–6*

My verse:

> *To open their eyes, and to turn them from darkness to light, and from the power of Satan unto God, that they may receive forgiveness of sins, and inheritance among them which are sanctified by faith that is in me.*
> *—Acts 26:18*

ACKNOWLEDGE HIM AND HIM ONLY

When Gary and I first got married, we lived in Memphis, and he was working for a company delivering beer. He left the house at four in the morning and would get home around ten at night. He wanted another job but didn't see it happening right away. He was not the type that took off work unless he was really sick.

One night, we were talking about how he looked forward to the weekends so he could spend time with the girls and me. I asked him if he really wanted a new job, and he said that he did, but he'd need to take time off to find one, and he had a family to provide for. I said, "Well, let's ask God to find you a new job because I don't believe He wants you delivering beer for a living." Gary knew it was wrong, but he really wasn't sure that God was the one we needed to talk to. He was thinking more along the lines of an employment agency. I was thinking much more powerful than that.

A couple of nights later, we were in bed, and the conversation came up again, so I asked, "Do you want to pray with me for a new job?" He said for me to go ahead and pray, so I got down beside our bed and asked God if He would bring Gary a new job. I was almost positive Gary did not believe that God could do what I had just prayed. But that was okay because I also asked that Gary would see God as the Giver of all things.

About two weeks had passed as I continued to pray for a new job when a phone call came. It was from an employment agency. I thought it strange that an agency was calling for him. The lady asked me if Gary was home. I told her no and that he was working very long hours and wouldn't be home before nine. She asked if she could leave her name and number and if I would have Gary call her in the morning. I let her know I would give him the information, and he would contact her.

When Gary got home, I asked him if he had gone to an employment agency. He said that he had not and was surprised one had called him, but he would make sure he called her back. I thought that maybe his name was pulled out of the files from recent visits to the unemployment office for a job. No matter how his name was called, I was praying it was the perfect opportunity for him. He got up the next day and went to work. I could not wait for him to come home and tell me about his conversation with the lady who called. When he got home, he told me that he had an appointment in Sardis, Mississippi, with a new Lawn-Boy lawnmower plant called OMC that needed a shipping and receiving clerk.

As it turned out, Gary's brother Ricky knew the lady who had called. Ricky was an engineer, and she'd helped him find many jobs throughout his lifetime. She was talking to Ricky and happened to mention a position she needed to fill at OMC. Ricky, not knowing anything about Gary wanting a different job, told her that he had a brother she just might want to call. Ricky knew Gary was qualified to do it; he just didn't know if he would make a move to Sardis.

Two weeks after we prayed together, Gary had a new job. He was driving from Memphis to Sardis every day until I could find us a house to move into. That was not an easy job, to say the least. But I was trying to do it on my own—in other words, I was not praying about it.

I would drop my oldest daughter, J'Anna, off at school for the day, and my youngest daughter, Montana, and I would take off to Sardis. I went to a realtor and asked if they could help us to find a home to rent, as we were not ready to buy at the time. A gentleman showed me house after house, day after day, that were literally not fit for anyone to live in. This went on for about two weeks. I was getting so discouraged, on top of aggravated, because the homes he was showing me were dumpsters, to speak kindly. And he wanted $300 a month for them. I was beginning to think we had just made a mistake, and this job may not have been from God after all. Isn't that just like Satan—trying to discourage you after God has done something wonderful in your life?

I was getting ready to go back to Sardis one morning when I got a phone call that my grandmother had passed away, so we were going to be driving back to Missouri for the funeral. I was sad and not in the best mood when I got to Sardis that day, and on top of that, the realtor was still showing me horrible places. In tears at the end of the day, I told him that if he wouldn't live in it or raise his children in the homes he was showing, then don't bother to show them to me. With that said, I walked away.

I was driving home when a thought came to me to go to the chamber of commerce and ask them if they knew of any homes for rent. I did not know why the chamber came to my mind. I had never heard of anyone going there to find a house, but I went anyway.

A friend watched Montana for me that day, and I was sure glad. I was so emotional with my grandmother passing away and having to go home without any hope of a house to rent in Sardis. On top of everything else, it was getting very expensive, driving back and forth every day and then packing things up and getting ready for the move in the evenings. I was getting overwhelmed! I found the chamber of commerce office, went inside, and talked to a very nice lady; she said every now and again, someone would let them know of a home for sale or rent. She knew of nothing at the time, however, but took my name and number in case something came up.

I got in the car and burst into tears—I just didn't think I could take much more. Suddenly, I cried out to God to forgive me. I had taken on this task without asking Him to help us find a house! I said, "Lord, I am not just asking You, but I'm begging You to help me." Yes, I was so thankful Montana was not in the car seeing my brokenness. I knew I had to get it together and drive myself home when, all of a sudden, a knock on my window made me look up. There stood the lady waving at me, in the rain, to come back into the office.

I went back in, and she was writing on a piece of paper the address and name of a lady she had just gotten off the phone with. She was telling me, as she wrote it all down, about a house for rent in Enid, about fifteen miles from Sardis. It was in the Enid Shores subdivision, had two bedrooms, and was $150 a month. I took the information and told her I would call, thanking her for coming out in the rain. She said she was glad she could help and to let her know if things didn't work out.

I got back in the car and thought the house couldn't be much at $150 a month. I had been looking at ghettos for twice that much. So when Gary got home, I told him about my day and let him know I was leaving in the morning for the funeral. He didn't feel he needed to take off since he had just started the new job, but he did ask me to give him the information, and he would see if he could go look at the house after work

I went back to Missouri for the funeral. It was a break for me to get everything off my mind and visit with my family. I got a phone call from Gary while I was there. He said he looked at the house and thought we better take it. I asked him if he was sure, and he said he thought we should. He wouldn't say what it looked like but said when we got home, he would take us to see it. The lady that was renting the house told Gary she would hold it until I got back and looked at it. I again asked Gary if he thought it would be fit for the girls to live in, and he said he thought so. I was just glad he had not rented it without me looking at it.

I got home Friday night, and we drove to Enid Saturday morning. When we pulled into the subdivision, it seemed pretty nice. There was a community pool, which was a plus. As we were going up and down hills, you could see many homes were vacation homes, and some were not. The road seemed never-ending, then all of a sudden, Gary pulled up to a house on stilts—you could have driven your car under it. My heart sank. Just what I thought—compared to what I had been looking at for $300 a month, that house won the "PIT AWARD." I was not raising my girls in a house on stilts.

I said, "Are you kidding? We can leave now; I have seen enough." Then he backed the car up and said that he was mistaken; that was not the house. Gary did it as a joke, but I was too nervous to laugh.

Soon he turned right and pulled into a house on the left. I could not believe my eyes. The house was so cute; it had a carport that Gary pulled under. He led us to the back of the house, where he had unlocked a walkout basement window, so we could get in and look. I could not believe my eyes. The basement had a living room, then a place for a washer and dryer, and a bathroom with a shower. I knew Gary would want that space as his very own. He took us upstairs, and there were two bedrooms, a long living room with a fireplace and window on each side of it, a kitchen and dining room combined, and a bath with a tub but no shower. I kept asking Gary if he heard the lady right on the price of the house, but then I remembered it was the same amount the lady at the chamber office said. It was a perfect house for us, so we rented it.

I am telling you—God is so wonderful. He is a loving and caring Father. He heard our prayers, and in two weeks, Gary had a new job. No one knew he was looking for a new job—no one but me, Gary, and God. And then the house: The minute I cried out to God at the chamber office, God was waiting to answer that prayer. He was just waiting for me to allow Him to work by calling upon His powerful name. I just stand in awe at how He goes before us and makes a way when there seems to be no way. He loves to show us He is working in our lives. He loves when we admit that without Him, we can do nothing.

Plain and simple, Christ loves us. The question is, do we love and trust Him enough to believe He is waiting for us at the end of each path He has prepared, or do we go our own way and never experience Christ's beautiful plan?

Father God Almighty, I pray the reader will acknowledge Your sovereign control over all things, especially their need for complete dependence on You. I pray they will humble themselves to wait for You to send blessings to their needs. AMEN.

> *Trust in the Lord with all thine heart; and lean not unto thine own understanding. In all thy ways acknowledge him, and he shall direct thy paths.*
> —*Proverbs 3:5–6*

Going Home

This is probably the hardest story of all to write, but I can tell you it brings me the greatest joy. In the end, God showed me He never left and was working it all out every step of the way—all the way to hearing my daddy say he was ready to go home.

God is really amazing. He literally took words that bothered me as a young girl when my dad said them and used those same words to give me complete peace when he spoke his last words to me.

When I was about eleven years old, I remember being in the living room with my parents, and a preacher was on the TV saying he could not wait to go home to heaven and be with Jesus. He was saying over and over how he couldn't wait to go home.

All of a sudden, my dad said, "Oh bull, going home, going home. If that preacher knew he was fixing to die, he would be kicking and screaming. That's a bunch of bull. Going home, going home, let me hear him preach that when he's dying." I remember thinking my dad needed to be quiet. Dad was a man of few words, so ranting like that was not something I had heard before. After that day, when any preacher would talk about going home to be with Jesus, I would think of my dad and pray for him.

My mother was saved in her thirties, and I can tell you when she received Christ, she lived her life to be pleasing to God every day. If she even thought something was wrong in the eyes of Christ, she would not do it or say it, and you could not make her. Before she became a Christian, family members said she cussed like a sailor and loved to drink a beer while she ironed clothes. The first time she drank after being saved, she got dizzy to the point that she had to go lie down. When she got up, she knew that was not what God wanted her to do, and she never drank again, except for one time. We were at a wedding reception when someone spiked the punch. My daughter J'Anna came over to where I was sitting and told me that someone spiked the punch, and my mother and sister were drinking it. I went over to their table and asked them how they were doing. They were giggling and said they were fine. I said, "Well, girls, you need to stop drinking the punch because someone spiked it."

Mother raised her hands up in the air and said, "THAT DIDN'T COUNT!" We had to laugh because we all knew what she was talking about.

My father, on the other hand, would go to church on holidays, but for the most part, he would take us to church Sunday, Sunday nights, and Wednesday nights but very rarely went steady for any length of time. But he always made sure we made it to church. Again, he was not a man who talked much—at home, anyway. But he was a hard worker. In fact, I would say he probably missed no more than two weeks of work his whole life. He was a good provider, and my mother was never in need of anything except the desire to have a faithful husband. Although they stayed married, being in their home, you would think everything was wonderful, but there was a lot of pain hidden in my mother's heart. She was determined to pray for my father's salvation because he was her only love.

Now my father and I had many talks throughout life about how his adultery needed to stop; it was affecting my mother's health. I caught Dad several times myself, but one time I remember in particular was the day God changed things.

I was working for a man and was going to the store for him. Now I had taken the same route to the store for three years, staying on the main highway that leads into town, never taking a back road. This was a spring day, with flowers and trees in bloom, so I thought I would take the back streets into town to get a glimpse of the beautiful azalea bushes, tulips, and pear trees that were in all their glory. As I sat at a stop sign, I saw my dad right in front of me on that narrow backstreet road. He was driving a truck, so I lifted my hand to wave hello at him. I was smiling and waving, but the look on his face was one of fear. Then I realized—with my hand still waving and my smile dropping to a shocked look—that it was not my dad's truck he was driving. Not only was that not his truck, but that was not my mother in the truck. Dad made his move and drove right past me, never taking his eyes off me, as I—still with my hand up—wanted to slap his face when he drove past me. I was sitting in the car wanting to do a 360 in the middle of the four-way stop, crash into that truck, and hurt someone as much as I was hurting. Instead, I started crying out to God, asking Him why He had me there at that moment. Never before had I ever taken a different road, and the one time I did, I saw my dad with another gal.

"Why, God? Why did I have to see that? You knew I would. You guide me every step. I need answers! Why, Lord? I don't understand." I was hurting so bad, but I had to continue my day and get back to my client.

For so long, my mother, sister, and I had been praying for my father's salvation. I had talked to him about it, and my sister had written him a letter. I was wondering when he was going to turn his life over to Christ. There was just something about Christ he was confused about. So I was not going to stop praying because as bad as it hurt to see him with another gal, it would hurt worse to know that if he died, he would spend eternity in hell.

A few weeks later was Easter Sunday, and Dad and Mother came to church with my family and me. That was the first time I had seen Dad since our little run-in. I hugged my mother when they arrived at church, and after that, I hugged my dad, but not without getting close to his ear and saying, "Dad, if I ever catch you with anyone else, there is going to be a wreck involved, and I promise you, someone is going to be badly injured, and it is not going to be me. DO YOU UNDERSTAND?"

"Yes, Sis, I understand," he replied.

I wasn't finished with my mother or my father, so I made a stop by their home a few weeks later. I had been praying hard for healing to fall upon their marriage. Although I did not tell my mother about seeing my dad because the thought every day was hard enough for her to live with. Even so, she never stopped praying for Dad.

So I made a stop at their house one day and told them we were going to have a talk. I was going to start the conversation first and without interruption, and after I was done, they could express their thoughts, and I would listen.

"I love you both with all my heart and wouldn't hurt you for anything in the world, but it is time for you to face a few facts about yourselves. It's a crying shame you have been playing house all these years without feeling loved. It would be a horrible day if one of you were to die, and the one left behind would always wonder if they were truly loved because you sure don't show love toward one another now. You are just showing courtesy to each other, with deep pain brewing inside you. You think you have everyone fooled, but you are just fooling yourselves, and that is the saddest part about it all." I took a breath and continued while Mother and Dad sat there with their heads bent. "Have you ever thought of saying you were sorry and walking away from hurting each other? When are you going to stop living in a house without talking or saying I love you? You neither one have many years left, so don't you think you could fall in love again?"

All of a sudden, my dad got up out of his recliner and walked over to the couch where my mother was sitting. He stood my mother up, hugged her, and said he was sorry. Mother said she was sorry too. There they stood, hugging and crying, as I stood watching and thanking God for putting the right words into my mouth. I could not have had the nerve to do it without Him.

Mother left the room, and I hugged and thanked my dad for what he had just done and hoped that it changed their lives for the better. He thanked me for coming by and said that everything was going to be all right.

I went and found my mother, and she was still crying. I went to hug her and tell her that I had to leave when she said, "Jeanie, I want to thank you for coming by and doing this for us today. Just the other day, I was listening to Charles Stanley, and he was preaching on the sanctity of marriage. After the message, I stood up in the living room, raised my hands to the Lord, and asked Him to heal our marriage. I didn't know how He was going to do it, but now I do. God sent you, and I know it wasn't an easy thing for you to do, but I want to thank you for doing it."

It wasn't long after that different people would ask me if my dad was okay since they hadn't seen him at the Legion anymore. Funny how God lets you know that things are changing, like running into Mom and Dad at Kmart. I spotted them several different times, and each time I would hide to watch them before approaching. Mom would be giggling at something Dad was saying to her. Yes, things were better between my parents, and love was in the air. Now if only my dad was saved. He was going to church with Mother now, but he had not made a choice to serve Christ.

Then came the day I got a phone call from my brother Keith, who said I needed to get to the hospital—Dad had been in a wreck. I was working, so I was almost two hours from the hospital where Dad was. I was told he was able to talk, but he had a large gash on his arm and could not walk. When I got to the hospital, they were working on sewing up the large gash in his arm.

After that, they sent him home in an ambulance because he could not walk. I still have a problem with that decision; the doctor said his knee was cracked but not broken, and there was nothing they could do about it. So we got Dad home and all set up with a hospital bed and planned to call his primary doctor the next day.

Early the next morning, Keith called me and said Dad had been breathing weird all night. I had him walk closer to Dad, so I could hear him. I then told Keith to call an ambulance and that I would meet them at the hospital. It ended up being a blood clot in the lung. That was a horrible day. The VA had the hospital transfer Dad to their facility, which was weird because they had no way to take care of my dad; they just were not equipped to help him in any way. So when he got to the VA, they said they were going to send him to St. Louis to the VA hospital, but they were waiting on a bed. So I stayed with my dad waiting patiently. Four hours later, my dad was gasping for every breath, and I went to see when they were getting my dad out of there. I got the same answer: waiting on a bed. I kept praying the whole time for my dad and for a bed to open up somewhere in St. Louis since they were now waiting on the third hospital to come up with a bed. Twelve hours had passed, and I lost it. I told my dad if he had ever prayed, he better start now because I was going to go get a state representative to get him out of there. And that is what I did. It was pouring down rain, and I stood on the steps of a state representative's home and asked him if he would get my daddy out of that hospital—and he so graciously did that for me.

When we got to the hospital in Cape Girardeau, Missouri, the doctors were so saddened by what my dad had been going through and told me they would do their very best to help him. There was barely a minute passed that I was not praying for my dad's salvation and for the doctors to be given wisdom. They had to put him on a ventilator, but he would not let them put him on any sedatives. He wanted to know what was going on at all times. The nurses were pretty amazed, but they said he would need something sooner or later. I guess they didn't know how strong-minded my daddy was because he was vented a total of three times in a seven-week period and was never on a sedative.

After being at the hospital for two weeks, I needed a place to get away to pray. I never stopped praying, it seemed, but I needed a hiding place badly. So I asked God to help me find an open door to a closet or just any place to lay prostrate and pray all alone. And there it was—a chapel. I didn't know who the huge statue was in the front of the room. All I knew was there was no one in the room. I had the whole place to myself. I went to the back of the aisle and lay in front of the last row of chairs; if someone did come in, they would not see me. I felt safe to pray, and I knew God and I were the only ones present. I had His full attention, and He had mine. I lay there for what seemed like an hour.

Him all to myself. His presence was very real to me, and to this day, the thought still brings me to tears.

One day after the nurse said they were going to try and take Dad off the ventilator in a couple of days, I got a call telling me he had pulled the vent tube completely out. I ran up to his room in the ICU, and there he was, smiling. I asked if it hurt when he pulled the tube out, and he said yes. Then I asked him why he did it, and he said he thought he was healed.

The doctor went ahead and moved him from the ICU room to a room on the fourth floor. He was on a BiPap machine and trying his best to let it do the work. We talked a little, but I told him to concentrate on getting better. I had the TV on in his room, trying to find something that he might watch. All of a sudden, I stopped on a channel that was showing a statue standing there in a room. I thought, "Where have I seen that statue before?" Oh my goodness, it was the chapel I was praying in, the one where I felt the presence of God. That room had a channel on TV all on its own for all to see. I laughed and thanked God again for our special time alone, or at least when I thought we were alone.

A few days went by, and it was clear they were going to have to put Dad back in ICU, and he was going back on the vent again. That was such a sad day, but he went back like a trooper, still not wanting any sedatives. He did have to have his hands tied until I was in the room for visitation, then I could release them for my stay. They didn't want him pulling the tube out again.

A few weeks later, they tried Dad out on the fourth floor again to see if he could breathe on his own. I knew deep in my heart that Dad was not going to make it, so it was time to have another talk with him about the Lord. I had noticed something different about my dad since the day he pulled the tube out, and I thought it weird that he said he did it because he thought he was healed. I prayed every day for my dad as I would leave our visit, for God to make Himself real to my daddy. We would hold hands, and he heard me pray for him four times a day. But now I didn't have to say, "Give me your hand, Daddy; I'm going to pray for you." Now he bent his elbow, having his hand ready to pray. It didn't dawn on me until we had our talk that day.

"Dad, I want you to know that I am taking care of your bills, and everything is okay. Mom has everything she needs at home. But that is not the most important thing here; do you have any idea what the most important thing here is, Dad?"

"That I walk down the aisle," he replied.

I looked at him and said, "What do you mean, walk down the aisle—did you get saved?"

Dad said, "Yes, I did."

In complete shock, I said, "No, you didn't!"

"Yes, I did!" he said.

"Did you ask God to forgive you of your sins?" I asked.

"Yes, I did!" he said.

"What did you say?" I asked.

"I asked God to forgive me for the grief I have caused your mother," my daddy said. "I asked God to forgive me for the grief I caused my children, and I asked God to forgive me for the grief I have caused other families because I have caused others grief also."

I stood there about to pop, then asked, "Did you ask Jesus to forgive you and to come into your heart and live?"

"YES, I DID, AND HE DID! But don't tell your mother. I want to surprise her when I walk down the aisle."

I said, "Well, Daddy, I have said you were the strongest man I know, staying under ventilation without a sedative, but now you are also the smartest man I know for realizing you needed Christ."

Time went on, and they were going to put my dad back on the vent for the third time. In his weakness, he held up his thumb and said, "GO HOME."

"Dad, I can't take you home," I replied.

He lifted up his thumb again, with all the strength he had, and said, "GO HOME."

Finally understanding, I asked him, "Daddy, do you want to go to heaven?"

And with the sweetest smile, he shook his head yes.

"Okay, Dad, you are GOING HOME!" I told the nurse that my dad was ready to go to heaven, and I called in my family, that were already home for Christmas. We all gathered around his bed and said our goodbyes as he drifted into GLORY.

My sister Penny, brother Keith, and I went to make the arrangements a few days later. I had a fear of going into the room with the caskets. I told the Lord I just could not do it. I believed if I walked into that room, it would take my breath away. So when the time came to pick out the casket, I told Penny and Keith that I felt I had done my part with Dad, but I was not going into that room; they would have to do it on their own. They got up and went to find the perfect one.

I stayed in my seat, and all of a sudden, I started thinking about the day my dad threw such a fit in the living room when that preacher was talking about going home. Then I realized those were the very last words that my dad actually said. *God had answered my prayers as that little girl.* And I thought of all the times my sister Penny and I would put our dad's name in a prayer box while we were on vacation, prayers for his salvation.

All of a sudden, Penny and Keith asked me to go into the room with the caskets; they said they wanted help. I said, "Lord, I cannot do this. I know I will pass out. I do not want to do this. Please help me!" I stood up, got to the door, and God led my eyes to a casket against the back wall. Standing in the doorway, I said, "It is the one straight ahead on the back wall. It says GOING HOME."

God answered every question for us—He showed that He was working it all out at the perfect time.

When my sister Penny got home, she received a phone call from Wanda Wyatt telling her how sorry she was that Dad had passed away. Wanda Wyatt and her husband were retired missionaries from my sister Penny's church. Penny said that her dad had gotten saved, and Mrs. Wyatt said she knew. She said Maurice Turney, a man who lived where Penny worked, had called and told Wanda and her husband Wendall that Penny's dad was in the hospital. The Wyatts had moved from the town in which Penny lived and had made a recent move to Cape, where Dad was in the hospital. So the Wyatts and the pastor from Cape First went many times to visit Dad, and by their faithfulness, Dad accepted Christ. I guess God made Himself real to Dad because that was the day he pulled the tube out of his mouth. I know he told me he did it because he thought he was healed. I never ever saw the Wyatts, but Keith said he had met them, and they were really nice and had come many times to see Dad.

Yes, Mr. Turney remembered the conversation with Penny and how she yearned for her dad to be saved.

How long do we continue in prayer for someone? Until they take their last breath.

I will be forever thankful for those true believers who know the true tragedy that faces those who don't know the Lord—thankful for their wisdom to cry out in a time of desperation for that lost soul, even if they never laid eyes on them. I thank God for the missionaries who are seeking one more soul, for that is our true reason to live.

Father God Almighty, I need that time alone with You, face-to-face; that is what excites me about heaven. Until then, I thank You for our encounters; my cup runneth over! You are all I need, and Your need is all I desire. Use me again so I can declare Your greatness! Amen.

> *Be careful for nothing; but in every thing by prayer and supplication with thanksgiving let your request be made known unto God. And the peace of God, which passeth all understanding, shall keep your hearts and minds through Christ Jesus.*
> *—Philippians 4:6–7*

LISTEN TO YOUR MOMMA

Sometimes the Lord tells you something so loud and clear it scares you, especially when the one He is telling you to protect won't listen. That is what happened to me one rainy morning.

I had just gotten my husband Gary fed and lunch packed and sent him off to work. I had my time alone with God reading my devotional, reading His Word, and spending time in prayer, and I was now ready to start my day. I heard my daughter Montana getting ready for work. I was headed for the laundry room but was stopped by an overpowering thought: *Montana is going to hydroplane.* The thought was very powerful in my mind. I knew in my heart that it was the Lord warning me about Montana, so I turned around and went to her bedroom and said, "Montana, I want you to call work and let them know you are going to be a little late; it is raining out there. You know that sweet voice of the Lord I get? Well, I just got it, and it was loud and clear that you were going to hydroplane."

She told me she would be okay. Again I told her to please call in and let them know that as soon as the rain let up, she would be there.

"I will be all right, Mom," she answered again. "I'll be really careful."

I told her I was not playing around; she was going to hydroplane, and she needed to take me seriously.

Well, she left for work, and I asked God to protect her, to keep her safe. It had not even been a full ten minutes, and I saw a red car pull outside our driveway. I saw Montana getting out of the passenger side of the car. Yep, she had hydroplaned, and it wasn't long after that when a state trooper was pulling into our drive. Montana went out to meet him with a big smile on her face.

I was behind her, and the first thing the officer asked her was why she was smiling. It was like he didn't like her big smile, but then I realized she had left the scene of an accident and had come home.

She told the officer, "Well, my momma begged for me not to leave this morning; she said I was going to hydroplane, but I wouldn't listen."

The trooper said, "Well, maybe the next time you will listen to your mother."

I made sure I told the officer that I knew the Lord gave me the warning, and that was why I begged her to stay home.

Montana didn't get a ticket that day, maybe because I told the officer we were going to buy four new tires on that car, hoping it would get better traction, which it did tremendously. I again am so thankful for the protection God gave—not just for Montana but also that her car was not wrecked because she just missed a sign.

I can't make anyone understand when God speaks to me, and I don't even try. I'm just thankful for the times that He does. I am thankful that He walks with me and talks with me and makes me feel I am His own.

Never forsake your time with God. To know a person better, you must spend time with them. May I ask, what kind of relationship do you want with God? To know Him is to seek Him through the reading of His wonderful Word, talking to Him and seeking His will for your life. He said if you draw close to Him, He will draw close to you.

> *Draw nigh to God, and he will draw nigh to you. Cleanse your hands, ye sinners; and purify your hearts, ye double minded.*
> —James 4:8

Who Was The Other Person

One night I had a dream that I was walking to a friend's house who lived across the street from where I went to high school. I was walking past the school, but something was drawing me inside. I walked up to the door and tried to get in; the door opened, and I saw a great brightness coming from the gym. When I entered the gym, I looked around, thinking I was alone, and saw another person at the other end of the room. I was drawn to the brightness of the room and started looking to see where the brightness was coming from. Then I looked up and saw the roof was gone, and Christ was elevated in all His glory. I could not take my eyes off Him. Although I could not see His face—it was too bright—I saw the scars on His hands and feet. There He was in a flowing white gown. I looked back to see if the other person was present, and they were. Then He spoke: "GO AND TELL EVERYONE YOU KNOW ABOUT MY LOVE FOR THEM BECAUSE I AM COMING SOON." His voice was so beautiful but powerful. And then I woke up and could not move in awe of how powerful that dream was to me.

I got out of bed and went into Mom's kitchen to tell her about what I had just dreamed. It was so real to me. After I told her the whole dream, she asked, "Who was the other person?" I told her I didn't know. I had looked back several times in my dream but couldn't even tell if it was a girl or a guy. Mom said I should have found out who it was.

"Mom, it was a dream," I said. "The light was very bright, and Christ was in the room. I was not that interested in anyone else."

"Well, I think it would be important to know who the other person was," she replied.

"Well, Mother, I think so too, but as I said, it was hard to keep my eyes off Jesus. He was the most important to me." It was so funny—every now and again, my mother would ask me if I had ever figured out the other person at the end of the gym. I would just laugh.

One day, about three months after my dream, I stopped by to see my mom. She told me I had mail on top of the china cabinet. I opened a letter that was from a classmate from school. As I got into reading it, I realized she was the other person at the end of the gym. She had the very same dream that I had, and I started crying.

My mother sat down beside me and asked me what was wrong. I handed her the letter and said that my classmate had the very same dream I had. She was writing because I was in her dream, so she felt like she needed to start with me first and ask if I knew the Lord. Mom was so excited that we finally knew, and she thought we needed to invite her over and talk about our dreams.

We invited my classmate over and listened to her story, and then I told her we had the very same dream—although I knew someone was in the room but didn't know who it was. She told me she and her husband were active in church and were foster parents. We departed that day determined to share Christ with all we came in contact with.

Years later, I was going to Job Corp with some members of our church. I started talking to a young lady, asking her where she was from. She told me she was from Malden, Missouri. I thought it very strange because it was my understanding kids in the surrounding areas were sent to another state so family or friends were not able to interfere with their progress. I explained it to her, and she said she was not originally from Malden, but she was living with foster parents there. I asked her what the foster parent's name was. When she told me, I got so excited to tell her about the dream.

"Let me tell you a story about your foster mother," I said.

As I was telling the story, the look on the girl's face kept changing.

When I got done, she said the foster mother had told her the very same story, but she didn't believe it. She said she thought the story was crazy.

I said, "No, sweetie, it is true, and I believe God is trying to let you know that He loves you and wants you to believe and obey Him. This is what I call a divine appointment. God is literally making Himself real to you. Even I am standing in amazement that He has brought us together. I believe God has something very special planned for your life, and I hope you know that. Why else would we have met?"

I asked her if she had ever asked Christ into her life. She said no and that she was not ready.

That day was a day I have never forgotten. I often have prayed for that young lady and have hoped she is living a bold Christian life leading others to Christ. Not long ago, I was at a store and ran into my classmate again. I continue to pray she finds a good Bible-believing church.

I have had several dreams that have changed my life. I thank God for that—it may have been the only way He could reach me at the time.

God, You are amazing. You go to great lengths to show Your love toward us. Thank You, and may those who read this story seek You and find You.

> *Trust in the Lord with all thine heart; and lean not unto thine own understanding. In all thy ways acknowledge him, and he shall direct thy paths.*
> *—Psalm 32:5–6*

It's Only Six Dollars Over

Every car Gary and I have ever owned was a complete gift from God. Our purchasing of cars has not been what we would like to have but what God would like for us to have. The process has been very easy, plain, and simple. We would sit at the kitchen table, look over our budget, and tell God what we could afford, and then we'd go to look for what He had for us. It's been the same routine every time, and God has been faithful without fail.

Gary was selling insurance, and he was on the road all the time. We were badly in need of a car, so we sat at the table and figured we could afford $100 a month. It wasn't much for a car, but little is much when God is in it.

We went out of town to a car dealership and told the salesman we were needing a car and had a station wagon to trade in. Our oldest daughter chimed in, "And it's a hoopty!"

The salesman said he would do his best to try to find a car for us that was low mileage and $100 a month.

A few days later, I was at work heating an asphalt pot off the side of the road outside of town. I looked up and saw Gary driving a Nissan down the road. He turned around and asked if I could run down the road with him and the salesman to test drive the car he had brought for us to try. Jerry, my foreman, told me to go ahead; he said he would watch the pot until I got back.

It was a really nice car, good on gas, very low mileage, and $106 dollars a month. There was no way I was going to say yes to that car. We told God we could only afford $100 a month, not $106. I got out of the car and told Gary we would need to talk about it after work.

I went back to the office for lunch with the asphalt crew. When I pulled into the office, Gary was sitting in the parking lot in the Nissan. I thought he had bought it for sure, but he assured me that the salesman was playing the puppy dog routine on us. You know, *try it for the weekend, and you will like it.*

I said, "Well, we need to talk about it because $106 a month is not what we told God." I went back into the office to eat lunch. The guys were asking if we were getting a new car. I told them the story, and for the rest of the afternoon, they told me I was crazy. They said it was a really nice car with everything we wanted, and I had to be nuts to walk away from such a great deal because of six bucks. I told them that I didn't care what they thought, but I was not going to buy a car for more than what I showed God we could afford. I told them my God was bigger than that, and six dollars might be Satan's way of tempting me to buy a lemon for a car.

In the meantime, Gary called my Uncle Gary, who was a car dealer and asked him about the real worth of the car. My Gary took that information back to the dealership and told them what he would give for the car. They figured out what the car would cost a month, and it was under $100.

All day long, I was told how crazy I was to worry about six bucks, but I didn't care what they thought because they literally did not know my God.

After work, Gary was sitting in the parking lot at work in the Nissan. He was all smiles.

One of my harassers said he would love to be a fly on the wall when I told Gary I did not want that car, and he walked over to the car with me as I approached Gary. Gary started telling me that he knew that I wasn't going to accept the $106 payment, so after lunch, he called my uncle, went back with the offer, and he bought the car for under $100 a month.

Smiling, I looked at my harasser and asked, "How do you like my new car?!"

We serve an awesome God. He is faithful—every time. What a privilege to carry everything to God in prayer!

> *But let him ask in faith, nothing wavering. For he that wavereth is like a wave of the sea driven with the wind and tossed. For let not that man think that he shall receive any thing of the Lord. A double minded man is unstable in all his ways.*
> *James 1:6–8*

Why Won't You Heal Me?

Sometimes God wants to heal or answer a certain prayer, but our hearts are not in the right place to receive it. Sometimes God wants to do a change in our hearts, but first, we must be willing to let Him.

Years ago, my daughter J'Anna had an operation to scrape a bone that was touching her brain and causing her great pain. She was not able to cough, sneeze, or laugh without having pain like a brain freeze. Years later, I had the same thing happen to me, and it was causing me great pain. I could not even bend down and pick up what I had dropped. I had to use a pickup stick to grab anything from the floor, or else Gary would pick it up for me. This went on every day for about eight months. I went to doctors all over the country. I had MRIs, spinal taps, and CAT scans. I saw doctors from Cape to St. Louis. This went on for so long, and it was not letting up. There were so many times I would be driving home from work, and I would cough or sneeze and have to pull over—sometimes for hours until the pain would leave so I could drive.

Gary put my socks on for me every morning and picked up everything I dropped without ever complaining.

I was now seeing a doctor in St. Louis, and he was running the same test I'd had over and over again, but this time he added a spinal tap. I really liked this doctor, but to tell you the truth, I was tired. I prayed for every doctor I went to see and prayed that this would be the one who would know what was wrong with me. I prayed for God to heal me. Not only was my head hurting, but I was walking on a torn knee that a doctor was treating as arthritis. I was paying for shots in my knee every three months that didn't help one little bit. But that doctor was supposed to be the best in Cape. On top of all that, I had also been seeing about six doctors for a problem that resulted from being given high doses of a steroid cream that was eating my skin up. Yep, eight months with three major problems, each one doing great damage to my nervous system and making my daily life miserable. Still working, I would always put on a smile for my clients and then cry as I walked back to my car, asking God to help me get my next client completed. I begged Him to heal me because I hurt so bad.

Gary and I were taking care of my mother at the time, and it had gotten where we could not leave her by herself anymore. We had a sweet lady named Henny that took care of Mother while I worked, but on the weekends, Gary and I took care of her. On Sundays, Gary would go to church while I stayed home with my mother.

On just another Sunday morning, I fixed breakfast while Gary got ready to go to church. Mother was still in bed sleeping. I got everything done, walked Gary to the door, kissed him goodbye, shut the door, and out of my mouth came anger. I shouted, "GOD, WE HAVE GOT TO TALK. WHY WON'T YOU HEAL ME? NO ONE KNOWS WHAT IS WRONG WITH ME, BUT YOU DO, AND YOU WON'T HEAL ME. AND I WANT TO KNOW WHY. WHY WON'T YOU HEAL ME?!"

All of a sudden, I started apologizing for speaking in such a hateful voice. Really, I don't even know how such words just came out of my mouth, but they had. I was too far to go back now. I fell on the couch and cried out to God to forgive me for my anger. "I am so sorry for yelling. You have to know that nothing was even on my mind to cause such anger. But since we are alone, and my mother is still in bed, I am asking You to tell me why I can't find out what is wrong with me and why You won't heal me. I can't leave until You tell me, Lord. My momma is going to be needing to get up, but I am not leaving until You give me an answer."

I was crying like a baby, praying and asking God to show me if there was any sin in me and to show me what was stopping my healing. Out of nowhere, God told me that I had hate in my heart for my father and mother-in-law. I knew immediately what He was talking about.

"Yes, Father, I do. And You know the reasons for my hate, but Lord, I would not let them see it. Even though they knew what I had to do to protect myself and my family, which they resented, I always treated them with respect even though it was the hardest thing I ever had to do for Gary's sake. Anytime I started saying remember when she did this, or he did that, I always kept it from Gary because I didn't want to hurt him. You know how they loved to show hate for me and my girls and the awful things they did to them. Do You remember how I would have to take two-year breaks from them because I didn't want to be around their hate for us?"

In the middle of my explanation, God reminded me that He was God, and I was not telling Him anything that He didn't already know. So I had to shut up and face the facts.

"Yes, Lord, I do have hate in my heart for them, even though Bonnie was the only one living. My hate was for them both, so I ask You, God, to forgive me. I am not going to tell Bonnie that I have hated her, but I am asking You to forgive me of the hate, and I will do my very best, asking for Your help to remove that hate because, Lord, I may have to take care of her someday, and I won't be able to do it without You putting love in my heart for her. I need You, Lord. Please forgive me."

It was so humbling when He let me know that He was God. And as a child of God, I needed to remember that I needed His grace myself every day.

The next morning, I was getting breakfast ready and dropped an egg. I started bending down to pick it up, and I thought, *Wow, I am already further than I have been in months, and my head is not throbbing*, so I continued bending until I heard a voice shouting, "Noooo! I will get it!" I turned my head, still bending completely over, and looked at Gary upside down.

He stopped dead in his tracks and said, "Babe, are you healed?"

I lifted up, with no pain whatsoever, and said, "Babe, sit down. I have to tell you something that happened as soon as you walked out the door to go to church." And I began telling him what had happened the day before, and then I asked him to forgive me. By then, Gary's brother had told him what his parents had done to our family and about things he knew, so he had to go through his own healing. He said he understood, and he forgave me and that he had to seek his own forgiveness.

After we had our talk, Gary said, "I sure hope you are healed."

"Why are you hoping for something that is already done?" I asked. "I am healed, so put your hope on something else. I am healed."

Soon, the end of the week arrived, and Gary let me know that he had told his mother that we were coming to see her and take her out for dinner on Saturday. When we arrived, Gary said he would use the restroom, and we would be ready to go eat. I sat down, and Bonnie sat right across from me and said, "Jeanie, how is your head doing?"

Now in all the eight months I suffered with the pain, she had never one time asked me about my head. A feeling of peace came over me, and I looked at Gary to see him nod his head as if telling me to tell her. So I asked her if she really wanted to know, and she said yes. So I started with my story, and when I got to the part where God said I had hate in my heart, hate for her and Abe, I asked her to forgive me.

"Well, I have never done anything to you," she said, "but I forgive you."

"Thank you." I felt Gary behind me with his hand on my back, and he said he was ready to go and eat.

We need to stop telling God we are not going to do something like I told God that I was not going to tell Bonnie that I hated her. It was God's plan for me to ask her for forgiveness. I did.

Sometimes it is the sin within us that holds God back from doing great things in our lives. He wants us to love like Him, to forgive like Him, and to seek His will, not ours.

To this day, it is a struggle for me to be around hateful people, but the Lord will give me an example of something I have done in my own life—that is when I am taken down from my pedestal, where I need to be.

Give it all to God—He knows the HEART.

> *Blessed is he whose transgression is forgiven, whose sin is covered. Blessed is the man unto whom the L*ORD *imputeth not iniquity, and in whose spirit there is no guile. When I kept silence, my bones waxed old through my roaring all the day long. For day and night thy hand was heavy upon me: my moisture is turned into the drought of summer. Selah.*
> *—Psalms 32:1–5*

GOD AND ALCOHOL DON'T MIX

I know people have their thoughts on alcohol and living a godly life. All I can say is you need to seriously ask God if it is His desire for you and your Christian walk and witness. Don't even go to your preacher and ask his opinion because I know many go to certain churches mainly because they believe in drinking. The pastor even drinks along with them, but not once have they ever asked God to reveal to them if drinking was a great example of a godly walk. How can it be?

I had a friend named Joe, who wasn't a friend at first. I worked with him in his home. I cooked and cleaned and took him wherever he wanted to go. Joe was an alcoholic. I knew that the very first day I worked for him.

Joe had just finished eating breakfast and told me to bring him his liquor bottle, a soda, and a glass of ice. I said, "No sir, I do not serve alcohol to my clients, and you will have to get that order all by yourself."

He laughed and said, "You don't know who I am, do you?"

"It doesn't matter who you are, who you know, or what you have or don't have," I replied. "I am here to do a job, and it is not to be your barmaid. I am here to do a job, and I will do it very well, above and beyond, but I will never hand you a drink."

"Well, you can cook, so I guess I will keep you for a while," Joe said.

"Well, Joe, don't ever forget this is a two-way street."

We had our ups and downs. It is hard working for a drunk, and he was my first. But we got along and had laughs along the way. But most of all, I knew he needed the Lord. I prayed for him and asked God to help me show him Christ.

Joe, at one time, had a lot of pull and clout where he was from. There were people who were actually afraid of him. I remember one day in particular, I had to run Joe to the hospital to get some test done. I dropped him off at the door while I went and parked the car. When I walked in the door, Joe was already seated, waiting on his name to be called, so I went and got a magazine and sat across from an older gentleman. I was looking at the magazine and soon heard Joe's name being called.

As soon as he left the room, the man across from me said, "Did you see that old man who just left? He is the biggest drunk in northeast Arkansas. He has hit every ditch in the surrounding forty miles. There isn't a ditch he hasn't been pulled out of. He ain't nothing but a wealthy drunk and has been that way his whole life."

The gentleman told me story after story as I sat there. Then all of a sudden, he said something that went right to my heart: "You know ole Joe had a Christian wife who prayed for him all the time, but I don't know how she put up with the drunk."

Soon Joe walked out and looked at me, then he asked if I was ready to go. The gentleman leaned forward and said, "Oh my gosh—you didn't tell me that you were with him!"

"Please don't worry," I said. "You didn't tell me anything I didn't already know except one thing. I didn't know he had a wife who prayed so faithfully for him. Why don't we continue that?"

I knew Joe's wife had died, but he never spoke of her. I was sad that she never saw Joe's salvation. The man actually knew that Joe's wife prayed for his salvation. Just the thought of that made me ask God, "How do I reach a drunk's soul?"

Life was not boring around Joe, to say the least. One day I was driving him home from a doctor's visit. We were at the state line, and there was a liquor store. Joe said, "Now I want you to stop at the store so I can get a few bottles of booze." I told him no, and I was not going to put liquor in my car. He said, "Well, drop me off, and I will call a buddy to take me home."

"I can't do that either. My job was to take you to the doctor and back home, and that is what I am going to do. Then you can call your buddy to take you to the store." He got so mad I thought he was going to jump out of the car just to make a point: that when he tells you to do something, you better do it.

When we got home, he said, "You need to leave. You are fired!"

And that is just what I did. After I left, I called my boss and let her know Joe had fired me and why. The next morning I got a call from my boss, and she asked me if I would go back. She said that Joe called her and said he was sorry and asked her to call me and see if I would come back and work for him. So I did.

It wasn't but a few days later that Joe asked me to sit down; he said he wanted to talk to me about something. He had a few questions for me, and he wanted me to tell him the truth.

I sat down across from him, and he blurted out: "Do you think I am going to heaven when I die?"

"Well, Joe, you tell me," I said. "You know the answer to that question better than I do."

"No," he responded. "I want to know if you think I am going to heaven when I die."

All of a sudden, the man that was at the hospital came to my mind, telling me Joe was the biggest drunk around. I cried out for God to help me. Then I said, "Joe, I want to ask you a question. If you died today, and you were laid out in your casket, what would those who knew you well say about you as they walked past your casket?"

Without hesitation, he said, "They would say I am the biggest drunk in Northeast Ark."

"Well, I do not believe alcohol and God mix."

Joe just sat in his chair, and not another word was said between us.

The next day, Joe was ready for me. As soon as I walked through the door, he said, "Come over here and have a seat. I have something to tell you. I told my daughter about our conversation, and she told me not to worry about it. She said I got saved when I was a little boy, and I will go to heaven."

"Well, that is great," I replied, "now I will go fix your breakfast if that is all you have to say."

"Well, what do you have to say about what my daughter said?"

I said I was not saying anything. I told him that it was between him and God and that I believed he knew the answer before he ever asked me in the first place.

A few weeks later, I went on vacation to see my sister Penny in Oklahoma. When we got home, there were many messages on my phone to call Joe's daughter. Joe was in the hospital, and he wanted to talk to me. I called his daughter, and she said Joe almost died, and he had been wanting to talk to me. I told her I would come by and see him after church the next day.

Gary, the girls, and I went to see Joe after church. Joe said hello to the girls and shook Gary's hand, then asked him if it would be okay for him to talk to me alone. Gary said that would be fine, and he and the girls went into the hall and waited on me.

Once they left, Joe said, "Jeanie, the doctors didn't think I was going to live. I almost died, and I even heard the doctors say they thought I was on my way out. All I could think of was our last conversation about heaven. I knew what my daughter said was a lie, but she didn't tell me the truth. Jeanie, I was hell-bound, and all I could hear in my head were your words: Alcohol and God don't mix. And I called to God to save this old fool's soul. I told Him if He would save me, I would never take another drink. I asked God to save me, and Jeanie—He did."

He paused for a moment and continued. "Jeanie, I want to thank you for not lying to me; my own daughter would have sent my soul to hell, but not you. You told me the truth, and I am so thankful you did.

"Now, Joe," I said, "don't you blame your daughter. When you die, you stand before God all by yourself, and you can't blame anyone but yourself. So don't blame your daughter for what you already knew."

"Well, thank you for not lying to me. Now I need you to make sure all the alcohol is out of sight. Throw it away—I don't want it anymore."

Joe was in his eighties, and he had been drinking since before he was old enough to buy it himself. I believe he said he started at the age of twelve. I continued to help him for two more years and then went to work for another home health agency. I would stop by often to see how he was doing, and he was always up to planting something or enjoying the sunshine. The last time I saw him, Gary took a picture of us, and we rejoiced that we would see each other again in heaven and how thankful he was that God took his desire for alcohol from him. He never took another drink since the day God saved him.

You know, I really didn't know if many in the forty-mile radius had ever heard Joe got saved. It was after his passing that I found out he went to be with the Lord. I had to laugh the day I stood at his monument in that little churchyard cemetery. I wondered just how many walked by his casket and said, "That was the biggest drunk in Northeast Ark." Then I thought of the day of his passing and how his wife rejoiced as Joe entered those gates of pearl and just had to thank God for His perfect divine appointments. We can't tell the whole world about Christ, but He knows who He has for us if we are only willing to live the Truth and tell the Truth.

> *Then will I sprinkle clean water upon you, and ye shall be clean: from all your filthiness, and from all your idols, will I cleanse you. A new heart also will I give you, and a new spirit will I put within you: and I will take away the stony heart out of your flesh, and I will give you an heart of flesh. And I will put my spirit within you, and cause you to walk in my statutes, and ye shall keep my judgments, and do them.*
> *—Ezekiel 36:25–27*

I beseech you therefore, brethren, by the mercies of God, that ye present your bodies a living sacrifice, holy, acceptable unto God, which is your reasonable service. And be not conformed to this world: but be ye transformed by the renewing of your mind, that ye may prove what is that good, and acceptable, and perfect, will of God.
—Romans 12:1–2

Know ye not that the unrighteous shall not inherit the kingdom of God? Be not deceived: neither fornicators, nor idolaters, nor adulterers, nor effeminate, nor abusers of themselves with mankind, Nor thieves, nor covetous, nor drunkards, nor revilers, nor extortioners, shall inherit the kingdom of God. And such were some of you: but ye are washed, but ye are sanctified, but ye are justified in the name of the Lord Jesus, and by the Spirit of our God.
—1 Corinthians 6:9–11

Just As I Am

I had a friend named Karen who was just like a sister to me. It doesn't seem possible that she went to be with the Lord twenty-four years ago. I have missed her so much.

Karen always said she wished she was born in another day and time. She had so much trouble relating to dishonest people. It seemed she had her share of dishonesty and trust issues with those who called her friend and family. For that reason, it was so hard for her to believe in a God. She would say if there is a God, and He wanted to be her Father, how could she know He would not bail out on her like her real dad did? She compared her earthly father to her Heavenly Father; she wasn't sure He would be around when she really needed Him or if God really could care for her.

Karen was the type of girl who put all her eggs in one basket. She had to trust you because she gave her all to that relationship or friendship. In many ways, we were alike. Friendship was not taken lightly, and it didn't take long being around a person to tell whether or not we wanted to invest our time or lives in them. But Karen and I knew we were going to be friends real quick.

It wasn't long in knowing Karen that I asked her if she knew the Lord. She told me she wasn't sure she believed in a God who would love her. She said she had been through so much disappointment and heartache that she wasn't sure there was a God. I knew then that she was not going to be the kind that you could throw the Good Book at—she was going to have to see God working, as well as the need for Him in her life.

Well, I didn't treat her any differently from any other friend in my life.

When I had a need, I would mention in conversation that I was asking God to help me or provide that need for me or another person. And when God answered that prayer, I would rejoice by telling her. Karen was so unfamiliar with answers to prayer that she would tell others I had a HOTLINE to God. I would laugh and say, "Karen, God is not a respecter of persons. He would love for you to trust Him to take care of your needs."

It got to where Karen would ask me to pray for a friend, and there were times that she would ask me to pray about a situation in her own life, and God was always so gracious to answer those prayers.

One day I told Karen we were in need of a car and that Gary and I sat down at the table together, figured out what we could afford, and asked God to help us find a car for $100 a month.

Now, being the friends we were, we had the freedom to say anything to each other without getting mad. She looked me straight in the eye and said, "You use God; you use God too much!" Now, it was clear by the look on her face—truthfully, a look that I had never seen before—that this had become serious, and I really didn't know what to say, so I cried out for God to help me to show Karen His love.

"Karen, I do not use God in the way you are referring. I would need Him if I had $500 a month to spend on a car. I would still want the car God has for us. God says you have not because you ask not. When have you ever heard me ask for anything that I didn't really need? I don't ask much for myself because God provides all I need. But when I do have a need, I am going to ask my Father to provide it. I would much rather have what He wants for me. You know, every car God has provided has lasted until they died without any trouble out of them. I don't try to keep up with the Joneses. I am perfectly happy with the car God provides. You, on the other hand, do as you please, never asking God to help you, and when you have it all in a mess, you come running to me to pray for you. Now that is using God. If you would give your life to Christ, no matter what came your way, you could trust God to help you through. He knows what tomorrow brings; we don't. So no, I don't use God. I just try to give Him my all, not just bits and pieces."

Karen started crying, and she said she was sorry. She said she just didn't understand how I had the confidence that God heard me every time I prayed. I told her that He never leaves me, and He never says He is too busy for me. God is our personal friend. Karen was getting closer to understanding God, but she had a fear of trusting in Him completely.

One day, Karen was driving past our high school and saw my daughter J'Anna standing in the rain, waiting on a lady that I had to pick her up after school. Karen pulled up and told J'Anna to get in her car. J'Anna asked Karen what the secret password was. Karen had no idea what J'Anna was talking about, so she told her again to get in the car.

J'Anna told her, "I can't unless you know the password."

It made Karen so mad, so she got out of her car and stood in the rain with J'Anna until her ride got there. When I got off work, Karen was sitting in my driveway, mad as a hornet. She said, "What is your password?!" Then she went on telling me what happened and how there was no way she was going to leave her alone standing in the rain. She said she didn't think she would need a password to get J'Anna in the car. J'Anna should have known she wanted to protect her, not hurt her.

I thanked her and told her the password, and said, "Truthfully, J'Anna was probably just messing with you, and I am sure it blew her away when you got out of your car and stood beside her. But, Karen, God probably would like to know your password. I mean, think of it: He has answered prayers for you and others; He has tried to get you to trust Him through the things He has done for you. But you won't let Him into your heart. I mean, what is it going to take for you to trust Him enough to let Him in your heart? But you wanted J'Anna to trust you."

Well, it wasn't long before Karen went to church with me. At the end of the service, the song leader led us in an invitation song. I was praying for Karen, and I opened my eyes and literally saw white knuckles squeezing the pew.

With a bent head on the back pew, Karen said, "If they sing 'Just As I Am,' I would go." Suddenly, the song leader, who never sang over two verses of an invitation song, and never changed the song completely, changed the song to "Just As I Am."

And Karen responded by walking down the aisle and accepting Christ as her Savior.

Karen and I were talking a few days later, and I was laughing, telling her that was the first time I had actually seen white knuckles. She said she was fighting it and just wanted the music to stop and get out of there. I said, "Yeah, it was just a miracle that the song leader changed the song right after you said you would go if they sang 'Just As I Am.' I mean, she could not have read your lips with your bent head and being on the back row—it would be impossible. That was definitely an act of God."

Karen looked at me with the strangest look and said, "I never said that." I said, "What are you talking about?"

She said that she never said she would go forward if they sang "Just As I Am."

Well, I still don't know what to say about that Sunday morning. I don't think we have to understand everything. All I know is what I heard and what happened. I know when Karen went home to be with the Lord, she was finally at home, and she was right where her heart had yearned to be her whole life. She is now where she can put all her eggs in one basket, she has the finest friends, and no one will ever steal from her or lie to her. Yep, Karen was always yearning for heaven; she just didn't know it until she got there.

The funny thing is at the cemetery, the day they laid her in the ground, we went back after the grave diggers were packing up, and I heard one of them say to the other, "Oh no, we forgot to turn her around, so her head was facing the east." I walked over to them and asked what had happened, and they said that Karen's feet were where her head should be.

I don't know, but it seemed about right for Karen to go to heaven feet first singing, "Just As I Am."

I never took a death so hard, and I never missed a friend so bad.

Thank You, Lord, for saving Karen's soul!

> *That if thou shalt confess with thy mouth the Lord Jesus, and shalt believe in thine heart that God raised him from the dead, thou shalt be saved. For with the heart man believeth unto righteousness; and with the mouth confession is made unto salvation.*
> *—Romans 10: 9–10*

God Knows The Desire Of Your Heart

My husband and best friend, Gary, means the world to me. He came into my life when I needed honesty, kindness, truth, and love. I was finding those traits in the Lord for the first time in my life. Then God sent Gary—not to take His place, but to give me more.

Gary has been a very hard worker and provider. I have seen him tackle life with patience and kindness. He came into our lives like he had always been in our lives. Gary took my two daughters and me with open arms. I knew he had another love, and that was playing the drums. He had been playing the drums since he was a young boy, even if it was on cardboard boxes from the store. He is now seventy and enjoys playing drums even more than he ever has.

There came a time in his life when he knew he had a desire to play, but his desire changed the kind of music he wanted to play. He knew he wanted to play for the Lord, and he knew he had to walk away from playing until he knew he could feel right about the music he was playing and the people he was playing with, even if he never played again. He didn't realize at the time, I don't think, that God wanted all of him, even if he never played drums again.

As the years went by, I could see Gary had given up on ever playing drums again. Although he would go out into the garage and play, that was as far as he got. I would ask him to go to the music store and put his name on their board for his desire to find a Christian band to play with, but he didn't feel comfortable doing that. Playing in a band is more than playing—the ones you are playing with mean everything. Gary had played with the same group, his brothers and sister, since he was a kid. They lived to play. They performed all over Missouri but mainly in Memphis for five years. Then lives and situations changed, people got married, and they got together now when they could. Gary played music with that group at our house every three months for at least fifteen years, but I could see that his desire was changing.

We were working on Friday nights at our church with an addiction program called Reformers Unanimous—RU for short. We loved praying for those who came and watching God change their lives. Even our prayer life together grew, and our hearts yearned for each and every one who came to our classes. We prayed for them, we cried for them, and at times God had us provide for them. We spent five years in RU, every Friday night, and I think we only missed five times in that five years, and that about killed us.

It had been at least five years since Gary had played with a band. He was getting closer to God and really had given up the thought of ever playing drums again. I was praying the whole time that God would allow him to play again with a Christian band. It really broke my heart for him because he never asked for anything; he is such a giver.

Gary had some guys who came to his class that were in a program like JOHN 3:16, but it was called Crossroads. Several times, a guy named Bobby would ask Gary if he would come to the Crossroads church at 4:00 on Sunday afternoon. Bobby had asked Gary to attend several times, so one day Gary said he would be there the next Sunday afternoon. I did not go, so I asked Gary to tell the story of what happened that day:

> The Crossroads church met in an old building in the old downtown. When I walked in, I could tell this wasn't a usual service. People were there from all walks of life, many with nothing but what they had on their backs.

Several were in smaller groups in different parts of the room, holding hands and praying. There were people from off the streets that were there to praise God. I was humbled, and my heart felt a spirit like never before.

When the praise band started, everyone stood up and praised God with a joyful spirit. There were a couple guitar players, a keyboard player, a bass guitar player, two female vocalists, and a drum set in the center with no drummer. I kept asking God, "Is this where you are leading me?"

After the service, I walked up and asked Jerry, the praise band leader and guitarist, if they had a drummer. He said sometimes but not very often, and the drums were his. I told him I'd played all my life and if they needed someone, I was available. He wanted to hear me play, so the band started playing another song while I played the drums. While I was playing, I saw the keyboard player smiling, and they were all smiling after the song. They looked at me and said, "Well, it looks like our prayers have been answered." I told them my prayers had been answered as well.

We have been together for over five years now, and I am now playing twice a week. I have seen God work in many lives and many lives changed. God has blessed me more than I deserve. He is so good to me.

Gary is so faithful, not just to Crossroads but he also plays on Tuesday nights at Cowboy Church. His walk with the Lord has been closer than it has ever been. God showed that first, and most importantly, nothing is to be desired more than your personal walk with Him. If you have lost something that meant everything to you, or if you feel like you are doing something that you know isn't pleasing to God, then walk away from it and walk toward God. Get closer to Him than you have ever been, and be willing to give it all up to know Him better. Revive your need for a deeper understanding of who God made you to be and crave His desire for your life. He knows best; He knows it all. That is when you find He is all you need.

Turn your eyes upon Jesus, and the things of this world will grow strangely dim.

> *But as it is written, Eye hath not seen, nor ear heard, neither have entered into the heart of man, the things which God hath prepared for them that love him.*
> *—1 Corinthians 2:9*

God, I Don't Have A Dollar Left To My Name

A friend came to mind as I was driving through her town one morning. I knew she and her husband were going through a hard time and needed to go out of town for doctor appointments later in the week. I didn't think I had much money with me, but I pulled into the grocery store anyway. Before I started digging in my purse, I asked God to help me supply them with some money to get groceries and gas money to get to their doctor appointments. After searching in my purse, I found about twenty-eight dollars.

I kept looking and found more money, then prayed for more. I looked in my console between the seats and under them and found sixty-two dollars. I said, "Lord, they will need at least thirty dollars for gas and something to eat while going to the doctor. I would like to get them more than a thirty-two-dollar gift card from the grocery store. Could you help me find some more money? If not, that will be okay; I will make sure they have at least twenty dollars for gas, and I will get them a forty-two-dollar gift card, and they can pack a lunch and take it with them."

I went through my purse again and a few nursing bags. I ended up with an eighty-dollar gift card and thirty dollars in cash for gas. I went into the store for a gift card, which they didn't have, but they made me one and signed it so it would be honored by the cashier. I thanked God for every penny He had found for me as I drove to my friend's house. After I dropped off the gift from God to my friend, I just had to stop and thank God for the wonderful gift I found in my car, purse, and nursing bags.

I was truly amazed, and then I said, "Lord, I don't have a dollar to my name, but I want to thank you that they will eat and get to their doctor appointment!" I then lifted up my purse to put it in the passenger seat, and there lay a clean, crisp one-dollar bill on my console. I had to laugh and call another friend to tell her what had just happened. We laughed in praise of God's goodness. God is so wonderful—try to never doubt His power.

> *A man's gift maketh room for him, and*
> *bringeth him before great men.*
> *—Proverbs 18:16*

God Made All Things New

There are times in our lives when God does a great restoration in our lives, and we think we are going to die—or we would just as soon die. But as we look back, we see God had His arms all around us. He was bringing us closer to Him than we had ever been because we had been away way too long.

When you go through those times, you look back and see where God made changes that you would have never changed. He removed friends that you would have never walked away from, and He replaced them with friends who knew your real need, and that was a closer walk with Jesus.

God is so amazing. Have you ever asked Him to use you for His glory? If you really mean it, He will do it. It is the most exciting life you will ever live, but it also has its heartbreaks, burdens, and disappointments along the way. When you don't think you can do what God is asking anymore, just hold on. Victory is on the way!

I have a friend named Kathy, who God put on my heart about ten years ago. I knew that there were things going on in her life, but I didn't know half the story; all I knew was God was putting her on my heart to spend time with her. And how I knew for sure was every time I left the town of Dexter headed toward Bernie, the thought would come to my mind to call Kathy to have lunch with her. I did that very thing over and over again, and she always gave me a reason that she couldn't, mostly because she or her husband were not feeling well. Again, I found myself fixing to drive through Bernie when the thought to call came into my mind as before, and I said to myself that I was not going to do it. The thought would just not leave, so I said, "Lord, I feel like You want me to see about Kathy, but, Lord, let's face it—I have called her eight different times, and she always says no, so I am not going to do this. I truly feel like You want me to, but I am not going to bug her."

God was not going to let me off the hook. I got off the road and pulled into the park and tried to make God understand that I just felt uncomfortable bugging her, and it wasn't going to work anyway. This went on for about thirty minutes, and I said, "Okay, God, I will call her one more time, but this is my last time. I will take it that she doesn't want me to bug her anymore."

I called Kathy and told her I was in Bernie and asked her if she would like to meet for lunch. She said she wasn't up to it—and I was thinking in my mind, *Okay, that was my last time*—when out of my mouth came, "Okay, I will bring lunch to you."

But she replied, "No, I will meet you at the restaurant!"

Wow, she was actually going to meet me, and I was thanking God!

It didn't take long, and I could tell Kathy was badly depressed. A lot had been going on in her life, and it seemed unending. Again and again, she had one disappointment after another. I started talking to her about the Lord and how her father, whom God had given her, was so special. How he raised her in the love of God and protected her from the things that were going on in her teen years. She felt like she missed out on those years, not being able to run the streets like most. On the other hand, I thought, "Oh, how I wished my dad would have cared for and protected me as a teenager."

We talked about so many things, and God gave me so much to pray about and ask Him to change in her life. At the time, I was meeting with some friends on the third Thursday of every month to pray for friends that were not going to church or needed the Lord. I asked Kathy if she would like to go with me and offered to pick her up. She agreed to go.

I called my good friend and prayer warrior Katrina to let her know that I was bringing Kathy with me to the prayer meeting and asked her to pray for Kathy, for she was in great need of prayers and friends. Katrina said she would be happy to pray for Kathy and welcome her to our prayer meeting.

I would try to check on Kathy every day. Each time I would find out how she was suffering, her losses were huge. She had been through cancer, and now she was suffering from seizures that had caused her to not be able to do her job. Kathy was a very good nurse, and she loved her job, but now she was not able to work. She had headaches all the time on top of the seizures. She was trying to get on disability, but that was not an easy task because of her age. She had friends who walked away because, well, who really knows why. It was really a sad situation that made no sense at all, kind of like fifth-grade girls fighting for friendships. Someone always gets hurt, and she was the one broken without any real answers. She had a son who walked out of her life because the money she once had, she had no more. He just took himself and her grandchildren out of her life. She and her husband were living on one income, and it was impossible to get the bills paid every month until she got approved for a disability check. *How much more could a person take*? I really didn't know. All I knew was she needed prayers and a friend.

It was about three months, and we could see God working things out little by little. He was answering prayers and showing her that there were many things that she needed to change so God could work, like trusting and obeying Him and getting in His Word and praying. I was driving Kathy home from our Thursday night prayer meeting, and as I pulled into her driveway, she busted out crying. I asked her what was wrong.

"The day you called me for lunch, and I refused," she said, "I was fixing to take my life. I had the pills laid out and everything. Then you said you would bring lunch to the house, so I said I would meet you because I thought if you came into the house, you would be able to sense what I was going to do. So I met you at the restaurant, and you talked about God and invited me to the prayer meeting, so when I got home, I changed my mind, and I am glad I did."

I was so blown away. I told her how I had pulled into the park and told

God that I was not going to call her again, but He wouldn't let my mind rest, so I told Him I would do it one more time. I told her I knew without a doubt that God wanted me to call her, but let's face it, that was my ninth try, and I was convinced it was going to be my last. I told her God loves her so much and wants to change her life for the better if she would only believe He can and will.

We cried and hugged, and she went into her house. On the way home, I found a place to pull over and park the car, so I could thank God for not letting me leave without calling Kathy that day. I thanked Him for understanding me so well, even when I was trying to say no to Him. And then I asked Him to forgive me for my arguing with Him; it was only that I wanted to be sure I was doing His will and not mine. And I thanked Him for what He had done and was going to do in both of our lives through this journey. Remember: Satan hates victories in Jesus.

Soon, Kathy finally got a disability check, and we were jumping for joy!

The next month, her husband died. *What is going on—how much more can a person take?* Was it ever going to end for her? I had seen God working, then Satan jumped in to ruin everything. No matter what, I knew nothing happens without God knowing it, even if we don't understand. Kathy's world was again turned upside down. I was hurting so bad for her, praying God would not let go and help make things right when everything seemed so wrong.

There were so many things Kathy was going through—many things from bad past decisions, like no life insurance on her or her husband—and now she was back to one income, credit card debt, house payment along with utilities and everyday needs, but not enough money to go around. Kathy had already tasted the goodness of the Lord, and she was going to keep putting her faith and trust in Christ.

Katrina stepped up to the plate again and helped get Kathy's finances in order by refinancing her house and getting her credit cards paid off. One year later, with prayer and walking closer to the Lord and trusting in Him instead of herself, Kathy was out of deep debt, and her faith was growing. Even though she was still having seizures, she was so much better. I told Katrina that I believed that worry was bringing on the seizures because Kathy would be fine until check time, and you could bet she would start having seizures and bad headaches—it never failed. I was praying for answers and for the seizures to stop. I hated that she had to take seventeen to thirty-one shots in her head every three months. Oh, she had so much to deal with each day.

Kathy met a man a few years after her husband passed and remarried. She was having seizures more often, it seemed. I was praying God would take them away and give her life back to her.

I was having some head problems, so I was going to go see Kathy's neurologist since she was a nurse, and I was sure he had to be a good one. WRONG! He was and is a quack. I told him what was going on with my head, and without one exam or touching me, he left the room and came back with a stack of pills, instructing me to increase the dosage each week. When I asked him what was wrong, he would not answer—he just said for me to take the pills. I looked at my husband and told the doctor I was not going to take any pills until he could tell me what was wrong, and then we left his office.

As soon as I got into our van, I called Kathy and said, "You are going to a quack, and if you don't stop going to him, he is going to kill you. You need to call your sister and see if she knows of a good neurologist around St. Louis."

Kathy asked me what he was giving me. I told her, and she said for me not to take it. He had her on the same pills, and she felt she was worse. She was on so many pills, and she was in no way getting better. I feared for her life, and I cried out to God to help my friend.

It wasn't long, and Kathy had a new doctor in St. Louis who put her in the hospital for a week to see what kind of seizures she was having. It turned out that Kathy was not having seizures at all; it was the medication she was on causing them. She was on pills that caused them and pills to stop them. It took some time to get the meds out of her system, and you could tell it was rough on her, but she just kept getting better and better. Her speech was getting better daily, and she carried on a conversation like she knew what she was talking about. Day by day, week by week, and month by month, she was getting her life back. And we were rejoicing unto the Lord, thanking God for giving her life back! She could now drive her car, something she had not done in almost a year.

The next thing I knew, she called and said she was going to work. She had a nursing job literally seven months after going to St. Louis and getting off the meds that she had been on for ten years.

God gave her life back, a husband who helped her from day one, and she dedicated her life back to the Lord. She is seeking God's will instead of her own will. Her husband got saved, and they joined a wonderful Bible-believing church. God gave her new friends and the ability to go back to work. But, most of all, God gave her hope when she thought no hope was available. God gave her love, a love she had never fully experienced, and God gave her a reason to live. Because He lives, she can face tomorrow.

Oh, I could fill in between each line with a ton of disappointments and joys in those ten years. There were even times I told God I could not do it anymore, but God reminded me that He didn't put Kathy in my life to give up. He was going to get the glory, and we were going to reap a closer walk with Him. God put Katrina right in the middle of the battle with us, and she joined in willingly. She was always praying, giving good advice, and always willing to give where needed. Katrina comes with a bonus, and that is her special daughter Kendra, one precious prayer warrior who takes over the throne with her pleas to God and prays with all her heart. I always say I would rather know Kendra is praying for me than anyone. We all have a friendship that will last into eternity with Christ.

Please know God hears and answers prayers. It may take ten years and going through struggles bigger than you think you can bear. You are right; that is why God says to cast all your cares upon Him. Please note you must trust Him to do His will in your life, pray and seek His Word daily, for

He has so much to tell you about yourself, and the answers are waiting in His Word. Obey Him, for fear is the greatest when we don't obey Him; He can't work without obedience. And as God works, I hope you are able to give to others that same hope given to you. Funny how God puts others in our path that need what we possess, the grace and mercy of God.

Remember, we are accountable to God, not our friends. Sometimes it takes us going through hardships because, although we say God exists, our actions say different things. Pride gets in the way and comes before a fall. Thank God He will deliver us when we cry out and turn our eyes, mind, and heart upon Jesus.

Thank You, Father, for Your Faithfulness to pick us up when we have no strength, for Your love when we don't even love ourselves, and for Your mercy and grace that I have learned to appreciate more as I have been humbled by both through this journey. Please continue to show me who I am and who You want me to be as I seek Your will daily. In the powerful name of Jesus, I pray, Amen.

> *How long wilt thou forget me, O LORD? for ever? how long wilt thou hide thy face from me? How long shall I take counsel in my soul, having sorrow in my heart daily? how long shall mine enemy be exalted over me? Consider and hear me, O LORD my God: lighten mine eyes, lest I sleep the sleep of death; Lest mine enemy say, I have prevailed against him; and those that trouble me rejoice when I am moved. But I have trusted in thy mercy; my heart shall rejoice in thy salvation. I will sing unto the LORD, because he hath dealt bountifully with me.*
> *—Psalms 13:1–6*

Humble yourselves therefore under the mighty hand of God, that he may exalt you in due time: Casting all your care upon him; for he careth for you. Be sober, be vigilant; because your adversary the devil, as a roaring lion, walketh about, seeking whom he may devour: Whom resist stedfast in the faith, knowing that the same afflictions are accomplished in your brethren that are in the world. But the God of all grace, who hath called us unto his eternal glory by Christ Jesus, after that ye have suffered a while, make you perfect, stablish, strengthen, settle you. To him be glory and dominion for ever and ever. Amen.
1 Peter 5:6–11

It's Your Child, So You Pray

I just believe when you ask someone to pray for a loved one, friend, or family member, you ought to be praying also. I have a habit of asking those who ask me to pray if they are also praying, and you would be surprised at those who say NO. They say they can't because they are too mad at them. May I say that I have been there, but then I think back at what a wicked wretch I have been, and that will knock me down from my pedestal.

One night I was up praying for the daughter of a friend named Glenda. Her daughter Terri was living in another country, and Glenda had not heard from her in years. She would hear from other family members about Terri and how her granddaughters were doing. It was a heartbreaking situation and really did need prayers. The country Terri was living in could be very dangerous for her, so I was more than happy to pray.

As I was up one night praying, the thought came to me that Glenda was not praying for her daughter. I got out of bed that night because I could not get Terri off my mind. I was trying to pray, but the thought that Glenda was not praying for her own daughter would not leave my mind, so I called her.

You could tell that Glenda was sleeping when she answered the phone. She said hello in a weak tone.

"Hey, this is Jeanie," I said. "Wake up—I need to ask you a question."

"It is 10:30," she answered. "Call me tomorrow. I am sleeping."

"No, you need to wake up. I want to ask you something, and I want you to tell me the truth. Do you pray for your daughter?"

There was a long pause.

I asked her again, "I want to know—do you pray for her?"

"I can't!" she responded, now sounding more awake.

"What do you mean you can't?" I asked.

"She has done too much, and I am too upset. I just can't pray for her."

Right then, I cried out to God and asked Him to help me because I was getting mad. I asked Him to put the right words in my mouth because I had a few things I was fixing to say, and I didn't feel very kind.

"I cannot believe you have been asking me if I have been praying for your daughter, but you have not been praying for her yourself," I started. "God gave her to you, that is your daughter, not mine, but I am up at 10:30 praying for her. And as I was praying, the thought that you were not praying would not leave my mind. I know that God gave me that thought, but I had to call and make sure. Glenda, how can you not pray for the wonderful gift God has given you? If you're not praying, besides me, who else do you think is praying for her? Truthfully, who do you know is praying for her?"

There was no reply.

"Are you listening to me?" I asked.

She said she was listening.

"Well, I think if you are not willing to pray, you should not ask me to pray. She is your wayward child, not mine, and that is all I have to say. I love you, Glenda, but you're not right in not praying for your daughter, and I really believe you are missing out on a lot of blessings by not doing so, as well as a lot of unanswered prayers. So that is all I have to say, and I am going to go now. I love you." I hung up the phone and prayed for Glenda—boy, did I ever pray.

The next morning I got a call from her, and she said when I hung up, she got so convicted. She broke down crying, asking God to forgive her and then started praying for her daughter with all her heart. "And guess what?" she asked. "At four this morning, my daughter called and asked if she could come home for a visit! She is coming home!"

We both cried and gave God the glory.

Does that not excite you? I sure hope it does. Every time I think of that night, I stand amazed at the presence of God. Our God is always present.

He hears and answers prayers. I hope you never forget that. Prayer and God's Word are the greatest powers that we have available to us, and we don't even believe in either like we should because, if we did, there would be changes in our lives and in the lives of our families.

I have noticed that the most difficult to pray for are the ones who their family says there is no hope for them. They want you to pray, but when you ask them if they are praying, they say no. You shouldn't ask me to pray if you are not willing to take on the burden with me. Please pray without ceasing, for God wants your faith to grow in Him. Where would you be if there were not those who prayed for you?

I see so many families struggle because they will talk about their loved ones in sin and ask for others to pray but will not pray themselves. I have seen the one in sin trying with everything they have over and over again, then watching as their family looks and laughs at them as soon as the one in sin leaves their presence. I have even seen it in church, wanting to scream out, "Why don't you all pray instead of snickering, and maybe her life will change?!"

I hope this story drops you to your knees in repentance to the only One who can change a life. I don't care what they have done or are doing. Never say never, never give up, and never stop praying—God manifests Himself when we pray!

> *The Lord is nigh unto all them that call upon him, to all that call upon him in truth.*
> *—Psalm 145:18*

GOD NEVER CEASES TO AMAZE ME

How many times have you driven past an old rundown house, seeing children playing outside, and said, "Lord, would You bless those little children somehow?" There are so many times God brings a need to our attention; some we can help, others we see from a distance, but everyone could use a call out to God for help. I did that very thing one day after church while I stood in line at the grocery store.

"Mommy, can we have some Little Debbies?" That was the cry of two little boys in the store that day. Their mother answered by saying no and then asked the cashier for two cartons of cigarettes. As the mother was checking out, with the boys behind her, they were opening up little candy trash cans and popping the candies in their mouths. As I was standing there watching the whole thing, I was thinking, *Lord, those boys are stealing, and I don't have the heart to report them. Would You please bless those children somehow?*

I was teaching a class of fifth and sixth graders on Wednesday nights, so I shared with them what happened at the store that week. I said, "How many of you would get Little Debbies if you asked your mother for them in the store?" They all raised their hands, and some said they would just put the Debbies in the cart. I said, "Well, there are children who are not as fortunate as you, and some are lucky if they get a real sit-down meal each day. I am just asking you to be more aware of those children in your school, say a kind word to them, smile and say hello, help them if you see them struggling, ask them to play basketball at recess, or invite them to church, but most of all, pray for them, and God will show you who to pray for." I told them prayer changes lives, they could change how a child feels about themselves, and they would make God's heart smile by showing them Jesus.

My class was collecting canned goods to take to a family in need for Thanksgiving. Ms. Beverly, who oversaw benevolence, gave me the name and address of the family my class was going to take a meal to. I drove to find the house, and as I turned a corner, I saw the address by the door and those two little boys from the store on the porch playing. I could not believe my eyes. I passed by the house because I had burst into tears when I saw those boys. I parked the car around the corner and started thanking God for His goodness, kindness, and sweetness in hearing and answering my prayers for those boys.

I went back and asked their mother if my class could come by on Wednesday and deliver a Thanksgiving meal to them, and she said that we could.

When I went back to my class the next week, I reminded the children about what we talked about the week before. A few told stories about being kinder to others in school. Then I told them that God was allowing us to bless those boys I had seen in the store. I told them about turning the corner and seeing those boys playing on the porch, and their home was the home that Ms. Beverly had given us to take our meal to. They all asked if I was going to get them Little Debbies, and I said, "Yes, one of every kind!"

Then one little girl spoke up and said, "I'm not going because that little boy pulls my hair in school!"

I said that I couldn't make her go but asked her to pray about it.

Wednesday came, everyone showed up, and off we went to deliver our meal. The mother and children were excited and thankful for all the food and the Debbies. The boy walked up and said he was not going to pull the little girl's hair again!

God moved in so many ways, taught us all so many lessons, and He showed us He is a God who hears and answers prayers.

> *And whatsoever ye shall ask in my name, that will I do, that the Father may be glorified in the Son.*
> *—John 14:13*

SADDEST DAY OF MY LIFE

What can stop us from telling others about Christ when hell is a breath away? I hope nothing ever stops me again. One precious life haunts me often, wondering if I gave my all.

I was caring for Becky, and was she ever sweet. She had one problem for sure, though—she didn't want anything to do with religion. Her daughters told me she would run anyone off who came to her door with the gospel. So as you can guess, I had to be careful how I shared Christ with her. Becky and I hit it off from day one. She was so sweet, and she made me laugh all the time. I would answer her questions about my life truthfully, and by doing so, I was able to tell her what the Lord had done in many situations. I was surprised she was okay with my stories. She didn't get mad or show anger at the name of Jesus; in fact, she listened like she had never heard such stories before, and she probably hadn't. I thanked God that He gave me opportunities to give her truth and was looking for the chance to go deeper with the gospel.

Then came Monday. I had not seen her in three days, and when I entered her daughter's home where Becky lived, I could tell a great difference in her appearance. Her daughter told me that Becky had been sitting at the kitchen table for three days, and she would not go to bed. There she was, sitting on a thick pillow with her head bent, leaning on folded arms on the table. I helped her with her bath at the table and asked her if I could put her to bed so she could rest better, but she said no.

"When I get ready to die, I will go to bed," she said, "and not until." Her daughters would get on each side of her to carry her to the bathroom and then carry her back to the bench at the table. They said she was not able to walk and had not walked in two days. Again I tried to get her to go to bed before I left, but she said she was not ready to die yet.

I saw a few more clients after seeing Becky that day, and when I got home, my husband, Gary, was on the phone with Becky's daughter. He gave me the phone, and she asked me to come back to her house. She said Becky was crying for her to get me to come back. I could hear Becky hollering my name over and over. I told her daughter I was on my way.

When I got there, Becky's head was laying down on the table. When I sat next to her, she raised her head and cried out, "TELL THEM TO STOP, TELL THEM TO LEAVE ME ALONE! MAKE THEM LEAVE! THEY ARE MEAN—HELP ME MAKE THEM GO AWAY!"

I literally felt the hair on my back rise, and all I could say was, "Call out to Jesus to save you. He will help you; call on Jesus."

All of a sudden, Becky stood on her feet and said, "YOU HAVE TO GO NOW!" She literally turned around, stood up, and started walking beside me. Her girls walked in and asked for her to sit down, but she said she was going to walk me to the door. They tried to pick her up, but she said she would walk. As we walked through the living room, she said, "I love you, but you must go." We could not take our eyes off each other.

I will never forget those black eyes following me as I backed out of the driveway and watched me as I turned the corner to never see her again.

When I got home, Gary was on the phone with Becky's daughter again. He gave me the phone, and she proceeded to tell me that when I turned the corner, her mother collapsed, and the girls caught her. They took her to the bathroom, and then they said she said she was ready to go to bed but wanted a Long John from the store down the road. She said she looked at her sister, told her to get a pizza, then turned around to ask Becky if she wanted anything else, and she had already passed away.

I felt like I had let God down. I wished I had fought for her, but there was a powerful presence in the home that day, and I only had the power to go so far because even her daughters didn't want the chaplain to come into the home and talk to Becky about Christ. But she called me. She knew I could help her, and she knew I cared for her, but she was not willing to do what I asked her to do—or did she? I do not know. All I know is God was with me, and He knew what was going on before I ever arrived. I was in the middle of a battle for some reason, and that is where God wanted me. I learned I must work harder before it gets that far again.

> *It is of the LORD's mercies that we are not consumed, because his compassions fail not. They are new every morning: great is thy faithfulness.*
> *—Lamentations 3:22-23*

> *And he said unto me, My grace is sufficient for thee: for my strength is made perfect in weakness. Most gladly therefore will I rather glory in my infirmities, that the power of Christ may rest upon me. Therefore I take pleasure in infirmities, in reproaches, in necessities, in persecutions, in distresses for Christ's sake: for when I am weak, then am I strong.*
> *—2 Corinthians 12:9–10*

GOD WILL PROTECT AND PROVIDE

When situations happen in your life, and you see that it is getting out of control fast, call upon the Lord right from the start. I don't know how long it will take for things to change, but I do know it will be worth the wait.

Your life and daily walk with God are the most vital aspects of achieving victory on any given day because the ultimate victory belongs to Christ Jesus. As children of God, we learn to fight our battles on our knees. I want to thank Jesus Christ, right from the start of this story, for giving victory to our bad situation.

Gary and I, along with our youngest daughter Montana, made the move from Arkansas to Wappapello, Missouri. We had anticipated the move for a few years, but we were waiting for Montana to graduate from high school before we made the jump. Gary and I made several trips to Poplar Bluff, Missouri, looking for the perfect place for us to buy. There was a house that Gary kept looking at in Wappapello, but it was too close to a bar for me, so in those two years of looking, we never drove to see it. Then came the day that Gary said the house was right at half the cost it was two years ago. We asked the realtor to set up an appointment so we could take a look. Praying long and hard for God to find us that perfect home, we knew that the home in Wappapello was the one for us after we saw it.

Poor Montana thought we had lost our minds in buying the house. First, it was roach-infested, it had a smell that would knock you down, and it was across from a bar. I knew how to get rid of roaches; the smell was coming from the built-in stove that was filthy, so as soon as we got rid of that, the smell was gone. Of course, the built-in oven had to go also—it had dead roaches in the clock and, I am sure, inside and out. The filth was bad, but the home was built very well and priced perfectly. The other thing wrong was the house: It was going to need a new septic system put in, and this is where the story begins.

Money was put into escrow at the bank for the new septic system when we bought the house. The realtor gave Gary the name of a guy he thought could do the job. The main thing about putting in the system was engineers were to be present during the whole process of putting it in. One day the guy came to put the system in, all ready to work, but the engineers were not present. On top of that, the guy said he had never put one of those systems in before. I let him know that he needed to contact the engineers and let them know he was ready to start. He said he had blueprints of the job.

When we returned from work in the evening, the guy had our yard pretty torn up. I asked where the engineers were, and he said he called, but they couldn't make it, so he started the job. He completed the job, and our yard had huge holes where dirt should have been put back in. He wanted his money, and we said not until our yard was put back level. The next day I drove by our house, and water was shooting out of the spouts that he had put in the ground. I pulled into the yard to see what was going on and saw that he had put some straw down. I thought he put dirt and then straw, but I found out differently when I walked on it and fell. That is when I realized he just filled the holes with straw and no dirt.

So he came to get paid, and we said, "NO, the system is not right; water is coming out of the pipes, and you did not put dirt back into the holes. Because of that, I hurt my back when I fell in a hole."

He did come back and put dirt in the holes, but the system was still not right. We were not going to pay until it was right. So he decided to take us to court.

In the meantime, we had to get the system fixed, so Gary talked to some guys who came in where he worked. Knowing they did that kind of work, he asked them if they would come by and take a look and see if they could fix our problem. They came by and said they were sure that they could fix the mess for $3,200. We had the money to fix it, exactly that amount—money we had put back to buy a used truck to haul wood in. In the meantime, we were praying for God to help us, as we were going to have to pay attorney fees, and only God knew what else was ahead of us.

I was driving while listening to Charles Stanley, a wonderful man of God who preaches truth. Dr. Stanley was telling a story about a friend who was in great need of money and went to Dr. Stanley to borrow the money needed from him. Now he was a great friend, so Dr. Stanley gave the money that he had saved to either purchase land to build a house or start building, so he gave it to his friend. It was not long before the friend let Dr. Stanley know that he was not going to pay back the money. That was quite a blow in more ways than one, and Dr. Stanley had to think long and hard about what to do. But by going to God in prayer, he decided to forgive his friend. He chose to love and forgive.

I had just passed my house while he was preaching, and I got to thinking it was not worth fighting over the septic system while we could get it fixed and be done with it. I pulled into a parking lot and said, "Lord, I am done. I will call Gary to meet me at the bank and sign off on the escrow, call the attorney and stop all proceedings, have Gary ask the men to come and fix our mess, and we will pay the $3,200. Just help me to forgive and forget. I know that is what You want me to do, Lord. Thank you."

I called Gary, and we went to the bank; the guy got paid, we gave all we had to get the system fixed, and all was well. A couple days later, Gary had an uncle pass away, and Gary's mother wanted his uncle's truck. Since Gary's name was on his parents' older truck, they gave the truck to us. We were so excited to get a truck. Gary was wondering what the truck was worth, so he went online and put the year, make, model, and mileage of the truck, and it came up that it was worth $3,200. We just had to laugh and praise God again for His help through it all.

That is not the end of the story, though. About fifteen years later, I had a nephew named Tyler, who came here from Oklahoma to get help through Crossroads, an addiction program. One of Tyler's jobs after graduating was working for the guy who messed up our sewer. Not only that, but the guy gave Tyler a trailer to live in rent-free for over a year until Tyler went back to Oklahoma. I talked to Tyler the other day and asked him a question that I wanted to ask long ago but didn't: Did that guy know you were our nephew? He said yes.

I have never run into that guy again, but I always said if I did, I would thank him for helping my nephew get back on his feet because Tyler went to work for another man during that time, but he was still given the trailer to live in. Tyler just paid the electric to the guy and did a few home improvements.

God is always at work. We think He doesn't have time for us, but I hope you see He is always working on your behalf, and He never leaves you or forsakes you. When you realize that, it will change your life, and you will give the glory to God. You will realize not who you are but who God is. Your life will never be the same! And it will be in those difficult times that you will learn to stay in prayer and not give up on God. Stay faithful and acknowledge His way, not yours. You will find yourself telling of His greatness.

> *But let him ask in faith, nothing wavering. For he that wavereth is like a wave of the sea driven with the wind and tossed. For let not that man think that he shall receive any thing of the Lord.*
> *—James 1:6–7*

TESTED, TRIED, AND TRUE

I would like to tell you I have been a perfect angel my whole life, but that would be a big fat lie. I have felt and fought the struggles of doing right and being wrong my whole life. But one day, God got ahold of me, and I knew I had to get right, stop believing the lies that Satan loved to hold me back with, and make the changes I knew God wanted to make in my life.

My biggest struggle was smoking marijuana. I started at twelve years old, and I loved it. I thought that I was not hurting anyone, and it made me relax. I just loved the feeling. It was the one thing I was going to keep from my past, and it was the one thing I refused to give up. After all, I didn't buy it often, and what I did buy would last me a long time. But every time I did, I felt so convicted. I would tell God I was sorry, I would tell Him I knew I needed to stop, but I really didn't want to, so He was going to have to take it from me if it wasn't pleasing to Him.

So many of us who are born again ask Christ to save our souls, but we really don't want Him to take away the things we enjoy. We really don't want Him to save us from the very things He needs out of our lives to have fellowship with us. We think more of fellowshipping with our friends doing those things we think we love than going to church on Sunday, thinking we are squeaky clean. I mean, really, do you go to church drunk, high, cussing, or smoking? Do you go to church and sit by the one you are committing adultery with? Do you go to church with a pornography book instead of the Holy Bible? The list goes on and on, and some of you might do those things still. But have you ever asked God to clean what is unclean in your life? Well, I did, and He was more than happy to give them to me one by one.

Friends were the hardest but were first on the list, along with smoking pot. Sometimes you have to walk away until God does a work in you so great that you can be around certain friends and not fall into the old habits God showed you were wrong—just until you are strong in the Lord so you can love them the way Christ loves them.

I knew that I had to give up smoking pot, but I barely had a friend that didn't smoke it. I am talking about friends from all walks of life, rich and poor. So I asked God to take my desire away if it was not pleasing to Him. I had friends who would say God made the plant, so it can't be wrong, but I never fell for that malarkey. In fact, I would say maybe you should leave God out of it until you ask Him to show you if it is of Him or not. That is exactly what I knew I had to do. So one night, I told God I knew the answer down deep, but if He made it plain to me, I would appreciate it: Was it wrong to smoke pot?

The very next time I smoked, I got deathly sick. I was throwing up and couldn't raise my head off the bed. A few days later, I thought I must have had a bug or something going around that made me so sick. A few weeks after that, I smoked again, and the same thing immediately happened. I was so sick, only this time I said, "Okay, God, I know smoking pot is not of You, and I will never do it again." And I can tell you I have never missed it at all.

One day a friend stopped by the house to spend a few days before traveling on to his destination. I came home from work and was a little upset about something that happened that day. My friend immediately said, "I have something that will mellow you out in the car; it is really good, and it only takes two puffs."

"No, that's okay," I replied. "I will be all right."

He said I would really like the pot, and it really only took two hits, and we would put it out and save it for later. I told him I didn't smoke anymore, and I had worked at my job for eight years and had never been drug tested. I told him I gave up smoking because God made it clear to me that it was wrong. He said they wouldn't drug test me at work. I said no.

The very next day, first thing that morning, I was drug tested at work. I can tell you that Jesus and I were rejoicing as the lady was reading my test. I know Christ was rewarding me with a wonderful victory in Him. I went home at the end of the day, got the Holy Bible, found our friend that was still there, put my hand on the Holy Bible, looked him in the eyes and said, "I GOT DRUG TESTED TODAY!"

I will never forget the look on his face. I am a big joker. I love pulling jokes on people, and I had pulled my share on my friend before, and that is why I had my hand on the Holy Bible. I wanted him to know that this was NO JOKE. "I could have lost my job today, and I would have hurt my family, my church would have been affected, and I don't know if I could have lived with myself after God showed me that it was wrong." Then I said, "When people say no, don't tempt them because I came so close to saying yes."

I will never forget the feeling I had that day, all day. God spent the whole day with me personally, and I rejoiced in His presence. He is always with me, and I know that, but there was something grander about that day.

Believe me, you are living your best life when you are living for Christ. To do that, you have to give Him your mind, heart, and soul. You will create a better life that honors Christ and brings you great joy! Just a closer walk with Christ should be our plea.

> *And be not conformed to this world: but be ye transformed by the renewing of your mind, that ye may prove what is that good, and acceptable, and perfect, will of God.*
> *—Romans 12:2*

God, Please Stop Her From Drowning

There are times God answers our prayers in seconds, and then there are times it may take years; it is up to us to never give up because He does answer.

Gary and I were taking care of my mother in our home. We took care of her for almost ten years. She never complained, and she was very easy and a joy to take care of. Mother had always been a woman who was so proud of everything that God gave her and trusted Him with all her heart. She had an operation one time, and everyone told her she would be in pain on the third day after the operation. She said she wasn't going to be in pain because she asked God to remove the pain on the third day, and she had no pain. There was only one thing I knew my mother feared, and that was drowning. She was a very clean woman, but she would not take a shower because she didn't want the water on her face. She always took a bath and would turn the water off with maybe six inches of water in the tub because she feared drowning.

I came home from work one day, not expecting what was going to happen next. Henny was Mother's caregiver while I worked, and she did a wonderful job. My mother loved her so much. Every day, Henny had notes written for me to let me know how Mother's blood pressure was doing and what she ate for the day. So when I got home, Henny was there to give me the update on Mother. As she was getting ready to leave, I raised Mother up in the bed, and she started gurgling immediately. I was so shocked to hear my mother trying to breathe, but instead, all I heard was the awful sound of her gurgling with every breath. I tried to pat her on the back while crying out to God to please stop my mother from drowning!

I was getting so scared; that sound was so familiar—I had heard the very same gurgling as I was present for some of my clients breathing their last breath. Mother was fixing to take her last breath, I knew that, but she couldn't drown. Things were happening so fast, and I knew I was going crazy because I was not expecting what was happening. My husband, Gary, and Henny were standing like me, not knowing what to do.

I fell into a chair that I kept by my mother's bed and cried out, "God, you have got to stop my mother from drowning; please don't let her drown. Father, you know she feared drowning, so please stop this from happening to her—please!!"

I got back up from the chair to try to help, and I watched Mother take a deep breath with NO GURGLING. She took another deep breath and then her last deep breath, clear as any breath could get.

I cried out, "She is gone, and she didn't drown!"

Gary held me, and we cried. Then the realization hit, and I said, "She is seeing the face of Jesus; oh my, she is in heaven. She has waited her whole life to enter heaven!"

Henny and I got Mother all cleaned up, put on her pretty pajamas, fixed her hair, and, oh yes, you must put on her makeup. Everything happened so fast that day. Mother was gone no more than ten minutes from the time I raised her up in her bed, and God stopped the gurgling immediately. It is a day that we will never forget.

Father God, I wait for the day I see You face-to-face to thank You again for hearing my cries over and over again throughout my whole life. I pray that the reader will call out to You to give them the power to fight unbelief. Help them to trust in Your Word and not in their emotions. Father, Your will is always best for our life, so help us to give You the authority to perform it. Amen.

> *Having a form of godliness, but denying the power thereof: from such turn away.*
> *—2 Timothy 3:5*

Mom, Were You Praying For Me?

There is no greater gift that you could give to your children and grandchildren that would be any more valuable than prayer. I can't even comprehend all of what God has done or protected my family from by praying for them. But I do know of times I felt the need to pray, even for others, and found out those prayers were needed. I thank God for the mysteries of His divine power of making me a part of something that He really had complete control over. He just wanted me to watch Him at work, like a spiritual communion that He chose to let me be a part of. I am always amazed and have a craving to watch Him do it again because lives are changed, God shines, and I get to tell of His greatness.

One day I was cleaning the house, and God put on my heart to stop working and go pray for my daughter J'Anna. As I was headed to my bedroom, I knocked on my daughter Montana's bedroom door and asked her to stop what she was doing and pray for her sister. Montana said she would, and I went to my bedroom to be alone with God and pray for her.

About thirty minutes after I came out of the bedroom, the phone rang, and Montana answered it. I heard her say, "Here, I will let you talk to Mom." I took the phone and asked J'Anna what was going on.

"Mom, have you been praying for me?" she asked.

I told her that the Lord put her on my heart, and I had been praying for her and asked Montana to pray also. I asked her if she was all right, and she told me she was, but if she had gone with some friends to get something to eat and drink, she would have probably gone through a windshield.

She had been at her friend Jamie's house, and some friends were going to town and asked her if she wanted to go. J'Anna said she would have had to sit on the console in the front seat because it was a small car. "The girl driving her car missed the road at the store and went headfirst into a ditch that went straight down," she explained, "and if I had gone with them, I would have gone through the windshield."

I don't mind telling you I stand in awe even today. Sometimes you don't get a response to your prayers—those prayers you prayed for others in faith that God heard, but you never knew how He answered or even if He did yet. Other times, you don't find out until years later that God answered your prayers.

One time in particular, Montana was leaving with a friend named Cory on his motorcycle, and I knew he had not had the bike long. When I saw her get on his bike, I flipped out, but it was too late to stop her; they were gone before I could get out the door. Fear flooded my whole body, and I cried out and asked God to protect my Montana. Years later, she told me a car had pulled out in front of them, and Cory tailspinned but kept control.

Montana had him stop so she could get off the bike. She said her legs were so wobbly she could hardly stand. She didn't get back on the bike but doesn't remember how she got home. All I knew for years was she made it home, and I remember thanking God that she did. It was over twenty years later that I was told what happened that day. That's God—always listening, always caring, always near, even if things would have turned out differently. God would still be God.

P-Praise Him

R-Repent to Him

A-Ask Him

Y-Yield yourself to Him

E-Exalt Him

R-Repeat

God wants to put hunger and thirst in you to trust, obey, and seek His greatness. Allow Him that control over you, for it is the beginning of wisdom.

Father, I pray You remove any pride, deception, or rebellion in our hearts that is keeping us from giving You complete control. Put Your words first in our lives and our children. Help our prayer time with you to be deliberate; help us to thirst for it and desire Your wisdom so we can discern between right and wrong and fear and revere You and only You. Strip us of our pride; in Your name, I pray. Amen.

> *"Again I say to you, That if two of you agree on earth as touching any thing that they shall ask, it shall be done for them of my Father which is in heaven. For where two or three have gathered together in my name, there am I in the midst of them."*
> —Matthew 18:19–20

Why Don't You Ask God For A Winter Coat

I taught a fifth- and sixth-grade children's class on Wednesday night at a church I had once attended. I wanted them to not only know God personally but also to know God hears and answers prayers. I wanted them to trust God and call out to Him for their needs in life. God wanted that for them also, and He proved it clearly in the story I am about to tell.

It was wintertime and very cold outside. One of the girls in my class asked me if I had a winter coat; she said she never saw me wear one. I told her I did not have a winter coat. She asked me why I didn't have one, and I told her that I just dress warm; a winter coat is bulky to me, and I would have to take it off before I got in a car because a coat was too hot and bulky. I would rather spend my money on something I needed.

She said, "Everyone needs a winter coat, and you might need one sometime." Then she asked, "Why don't you pray for one?"

"Maybe I will," I said.

I could tell it was a challenge, so I asked, "Why don't you pray that I find a coat also?" I knew she was putting me and prayer to the test.

After getting home from church, I asked God to help me find a coat I could afford. At the time, people were wearing down-filled coats that were around eighty dollars and up. I was not going to pay that much for a coat that I probably would not wear anyway. I just wanted God to show her that He cares about our needs.

A couple days later, I was walking into our Walmart store. As I was walking toward the doors, looking in the windows, I saw a teal green coat hanging in the ladies' department on a rack. I knew that coat was mine; I truly did. I was so sure I walked up, put it on, and it fit perfectly. I then looked for the price tag, and what I saw just blew me away. The coat had a Burlington Coat Factory label on the sleeve that said eighty dollars and a Walmart tag that said twenty-five dollars. I took the coat to the information desk and said I didn't know they carried Burlington Coat Factory products and was wondering if there was a mistake in the price.

She looked at the coat and said the price was correct and that sometimes they get stuff from other stores in their trucks, so they discount the price and sell it anyway. Not only did God find me a coat I could afford, but He gave me one I really liked!

I put the tags in the coat pocket and wore it to church the next Sunday. Boy, was that girl surprised when I wore a coat to class that night! I asked her if she liked my new coat. She said she really did, and I then proceeded to tell her the story. Then I pulled the coat tags out of my pocket and showed her the price of the coat. She could not believe I got the coat for twenty-five dollars. I thanked her for praying for me, but I could tell by the look on her face that she didn't pray for me, so she didn't reply.

About seven years later, we moved to another town, and that same girl and her friend came to our home, stopping by to see our daughter Montana. I went out to greet them, and out of the blue, the girl asked me if I still had that winter coat. I said I did and went and got it for her.

"I started to sell the coat several times in a yard sale because I don't wear it," I told her, "but I couldn't part with it, only because it was so sweet how God had it waiting for me. In fact, I saw it before I even entered the store. God showed me the coat through the glass window, and I knew it was there just for me. God is so good like that. I am surprised that you remembered the coat, but I am glad you did."

The girls were in a hurry, so I did not have the chance to ask her if she was trusting God to provide for her needs. I pray for her even today—that I do know—to give it all to Jesus and surrender her all to Him, and I pray that she has.

Never underestimate what God can do. He knows your heart, but He wants you to know His.

Father, the needs are many for those who have read this story. I pray it is for Your glory that they ask You to provide their every need. I pray they will be at peace with what You provide and praise You for what You did not allow. Give them the wisdom to wait for Your answer. Show them how, Lord; teach them to trust and obey Your Word. Humble them as they seek You in all Your glory. I pray they will declare Your greatness. I pray they will not be able to keep such wonderful love for themselves, but they will help others to crave Your attention in their lives so they will walk in Your will for their lives and not their own. In Your precious name, name above all names, in the name of Jesus, I pray. Amen.

> *But without faith it is impossible to please him: for he that cometh to God must believe that he is, and that he is a rewarder of them that diligently seek him.*
> *—Hebrew 11:6*

IF I DIE BEFORE YOU COME BACK, JUST KNOW I WENT TO HEAVEN

I always knew that I had a job to do each and every day, and that was to make sure my clients knew the Lord. I was put in front of them for that reason, and I knew God, who lives inside of me, would give me the right words to say. It was not always easy, but I knew I had to do my very best to show them Christ. God was the one working through me because I could not have done it on my own. I cried out for Him to help me constantly.

And then I met Sly, who knew just enough of the Bible to confuse me as to why he would deny it. He was a challenge, but God . . .

Sly was a slick one, and he had questions about my feelings on different subjects. Then he would try to convince me that I could be wrong in my thinking. So I would have to quote God's Word to him so he would know that I only believe the way I do because God said it to be that way. Then he would try to convince me that maybe I was interpreting the Bible wrong, so I would show him what the Bible said on the subject and ask, "How would you say it should be interpreted?" Then he would agree with me or, rather, with God's Word. Sly loved to talk about the Bible and ask me what I thought on one subject or another. It seemed he was ready for me with more questions each visit.

One day I was leaving, and his wife asked me, "Did I hear you and Sly talking about God?" I said yes and asked her why she asked because her face was in shock. She told me that they used to have Bible study in their home with others and that Sly used to teach a Sunday school class. One Sunday, after teaching and completing Revelations, however, he came home and threw his Bible in the trash and told her she was not to speak the name of Jesus around him anymore. Well, she was not about to give up her Jesus no matter what he said. So she stayed in the den, and he stayed in his office each day after work without talking a whole lot to each other for twenty years.

I could not believe my ears. She was so amazed that he was allowing any talk about Jesus, and she was hoping our talks would continue because Sly needed to get things right with the Lord.

When I got in the car after talking to Sly's wife, I asked God to help me. I felt overwhelmed by what I had just heard, and, to tell you the truth, I was a little scared. Sly, I was sure, knew more than I did about the Lord and all of a sudden, it was like he was putting me to the test—almost like he was checking me out to see if I really believed and if I would stand firm on my belief in God's Word. It was as if he wanted me to back down on my convictions, to compromise a little. But God had already done a work in my life on each subject, so I not only showed him in God's Word why I believe the way I do, but I had a story of how God showed me it was right or wrong. His wife really got me praying and asking God to help me understand what was going on with Sly. And I wanted to know why he threw his Bible in the trash, a question I couldn't ask because he didn't tell me—his wife did—and she didn't want him to know we talked.

I saved Sly as my last client for the day. His whole life had changed, and, being a farmer, he still wanted to watch things grow, so I would stay after work and help him in his little greenhouse. I would do things he just didn't have the strength to do. He loved starting plants from seeds so his wife could plant them in her yard, which she loved doing. We would have our talks constantly about God, and he would ask me why I believed what I believed, and I would tell him. Soon, I started asking him what he believed. To many of his answers, I would respond, "Now, Sly, you are an intelligent man, and you know better than that," or I would say, "I do not believe you believe what you just said; there is no way you believe that." He would chuckle, and I would shake my head.

One day, I was getting ready to leave, and he said, "Hey, I just wanted you to know, if I die before you come back, just know I went to heaven."

I stopped at the door and said, "Well, that's good to know. Thanks for telling me; did you tell your wife?"

"No," he replied.

"Well, maybe you should," I responded. "I am sure she would be glad to hear that from you."

Sly and his wife would meet in the kitchen when people would come to visit, but Sly would not go in the den; it didn't matter if they were home alone or if they had company. I asked God to mend their marriage and their time together. They were twenty years living in the same house but living separately, and I knew that was not how God wanted them to live. There was the Bible in the trash that no one knew the answer to, so I felt that he had asked me enough questions, and it was time he answered one for me. The only problem was—he didn't know I knew.

One day, Sly, his wife, and I were in the kitchen. It was always a joy talking to them together, and you would have never guessed they lived their lives as they did. I was getting ready to leave, and the thought came to me to ask Sly why he threw his Bible in the trash, so I did.

"Sly, I want to ask you a question. You can tell me now, or you can tell me later, but I would like to know why you threw your Bible in the trash."

His wife chimed in, "Yes, I would like to know also."

"I will tell you now," he said. "I had just finished teaching the book of Revelation, and I realized the people were the same as they have always been, one way at church and another way the rest of the week. The Bible was not changing anyone's life, including mine. So I came home and threw it away."

I reminded him that he told me if he died before I came back, he would be in heaven. I asked him if that was true, and he said yes, it was—that he got things right with God. So I said, "Well, you and your wife have wasted many years apart, and it is time you two started praying together for your family and for each other. It is time to get it right and do it right."

They started praying that night together and saw many prayers answered with the time they had left together before the Lord took Sly home. It was about a year that God allowed me and Sly to have our talks. I do believe that he was putting me to the test to see if my talk matched my walk, but I didn't realize that until I found out why he threw his Bible away. He had the best example he could have ever asked for in his wife—she walked the walk, she talked the talk, and she did not allow him to take her God away from her. She would not walk away from the only One who could turn Sly's life around.

I thank God for the time I had with that family and still do have. Sly's wife and I are the best of friends; we go on road trips junking together, we pray together, we go out to eat together, and I cherish every moment I have with her. We carry one another's burdens, and we can't stop talking of the goodness of God!

Lord, help me to not be afraid of those who seem different from me. Show me how to show Your love, grace, and forgiveness that they so desperately need in their life. Help me to stand firm by putting on the full armor of God. Amen.

> *Seeing ye have purified your souls in obeying the truth through the Spirit unto unfeigned love of the brethren, see that ye love one another with a pure heart fervently: Being born again, not of corruptible seed, but of incorruptible, by the word of God, which liveth and abideth forever. For All flesh is as grass, And all the glory of man as the flower of grass. The grass withereth, and the flower thereof falleth away: But the word of the Lord endureth for ever. And this is the word which by the gospel is preached unto you.*
> —1 Peter 1:22–25

Happy Anniversary

When you work in home health, every day is new and has its challenges. I knew God was leading me each and every day. God had His reason for having me in each home, seeing that particular client, and I knew what I had to do—just show them Jesus, and He would guide me through.

Farmer Brown was one of the craziest care experiences I had been assigned. He was brought home to die from a nursing home. He'd stopped eating and was very weak, so his wife let him come home to die. Mr. Brown had cancer and was left with a colostomy bag, but that was it. There was no reason he should not be back on his feet, but his wife had him go to a nursing home to heal, and the nursing home let him lie in bed for three months without exercise of any kind. So he turned to mush and was ready to die.

When I started seeing him in his home, he was angry. Therapy came for only a short period of time, and they said that was all Medicare would allow in physical therapy visits. His wife hired a caregiver so she could still work, and he was stuck in the back of the house in his bedroom while life went on without him. At night his wife stayed in the front of the house, only entering his room to bring him something to eat.

One day, he broke down and told me his wife wanted him dead. He said at age forty, she moved into another bedroom, and they lived separate lives. He didn't like it, but that was what she wanted. He said he lived like that until age sixty, then he started visiting a bar and dating a gal he really liked and enjoyed being around. He said his wife found out but was not going to leave him, so they lived separate lives in the same house.

One day I asked Mr. Brown if he was walking and getting around well before his surgery. He said he was walking fine and getting around well, then he had the surgery and was put in the nursing home so he could heal from the inside out. They never exercised him; he just lay in bed day after day for three months, which left him with no strength in his legs or body. My heart just broke, so I decided that while he was my client, I was going to do my best to help get his strength back. I left that day asking God to help me, to show me what I could do and how to do it.

On the next visit, I told Mr. Brown that I would like to help him to get his strength back and hopefully get him walking again; if he wanted me to, I would be happy to try. I didn't expect his answer.

"Oh, you think you can do anything, don't you?" he replied. "You think you are so smart. Well, there are things you can't do."

Surprised, I responded, "Well, at least I am offering, but I can promise you one thing: I am asking if you want me to help, so if you don't tell me yes or no today, you can beg me to help you tomorrow, and I will tell you NO. So you make up your mind and let me know before I leave, and I will not mention it again."

He didn't say much that day, and I was getting ready to go, putting my bag on my shoulder, when he finally spoke.

"I thought you were going to help me," he said sarcastically.

I put my bag down and started working on his leg strength.

Time was clicking right along, and Mr. Brown was getting stronger day by day. He did not want his wife to know about his progress at all; in fact, she didn't even know he was getting any form of exercise. I knew it was going to be soon that I would be calling to have him evaluated again for therapy because he needed help with getting up and down the stairs. He had been working hard for three months. In fact, he was enjoying walking through the house and watching TV in his favorite chair, but when it was time for his wife to come home, he would jump back into bed.

The day came when the therapist came out to the house and made arrangements for Mr. Brown to go to rehab for four weeks. He said he would let his wife know and get things ready to go the next day. I helped him get packed for the trip.

As he was telling me what to pack, I stopped and said, "Now, Mr. Brown, I haven't helped you to walk so that you will start going to the bar again. In fact, I am going to pray that if you do, you will have a wreck."

"Well, then I will just walk there."

"Then I will pray for a drunk driver to run up on the sidewalk and run over you."

"I believe you would really pray for that," he said, laughing.

"Mr. Brown, through all this time we have been together, through all our talks about the Lord, I truly hope and pray you have seen Christ and His love for you in giving you a second chance. I pray you receive His forgiveness and learn to forgive yourself. I would hate to know this time was all in vain because what really matters most is that you see Christ's love for you. I hope more than walking physically, you start walking spiritually with the Lord."

He said he thought along those lines every day and thanked me for telling him about Jesus. He knew he needed to get back in church, and he would work on that. He then asked me to go out to his fishing bus and get the envelope from under the seventh seat on the left. He told me when his wife found out he could walk and was going to therapy, she would get rid of his bus for spite.

When I came into the room with his envelope, he asked me how much money was in it. I told him I didn't know any money was in it. He said to open it and count the money for him. There was $8,400, then he asked me to take it home with me until he got back home. I told him that I could not and would not be responsible for his money. He asked what he could do with the money because he had no place to put it. He knew when he came back home, his wife would be gone and take everything in the house. I asked him if she would take his bedroom suite, and he said no. So I said I would tape the envelope behind his dresser.

The next morning, I entered his house to find his wife, son, and daughter sitting at the kitchen table. They were mad as a hornet but didn't say a word to me. When I went into his room, he started laughing and told me the story about getting out of his bed and walking into the living room to tell his wife he was going to therapy in the morning. He said their air conditioner had gone out last night, so she came and got his stand-up fan from his bedroom and left him with no air. He said he waited about an hour, then got out of bed and walked up behind her while she was sitting in her chair with two fans blowing on her. When he got to the side of her chair, he said, "I will be going to rehab in the morning, and I have come to get my fan." She about jumped out of her chair and looked like she just saw a ghost.

Mr. Brown said his wife was really mad at me because I did not tell her I was helping him to walk. He said she called my boss that morning to report me, but my boss told her I was asked by the patient not to tell, so I could have been in trouble if I'd told her. When Mr. Brown came back home, he did not need home health, so I never saw him again.

A year later, I received a phone call, and the voice said, "Happy Anniversary!"

The caller identified himself as Mr. Brown, and he said it was a year ago that day I convinced him I cared enough to help him walk again. He told me that when he got home, his wife had moved to Florida, his children had sold some of his land, and he had a letter waiting on him from a lawyer saying he was incompetent. He'd since got his land back, and his daughter had to come up with a bunch of money for all she had done in forging his name. He said he had just bought him and his girlfriend jogging suits and a treadmill, and now he wanted to buy me anything I wanted. He asked me if I needed a new car, then told me to name it, and he would get it.

"Do you mean that?"

He said yes.

"Okay, then, I want you to get on that treadmill, stay healthy, and go to church. There is nothing material you can buy me that would make me any happier."

He told me he was working on both. He had not been back to the bar, and his girlfriend was not working there anymore. His divorce was soon to be over, and he was looking for a church. I told him that my hope for him from the start was for him to accept Christ as his Lord and Savior. He told me he knew that and had not forgotten our talks or how I had helped him.

Mr. Brown lived for six more years, and I never knew if he asked the Lord into his heart—that would have been a call I would have loved to have received. After all, he told me that he would give me anything I wanted!

> *To open their eyes, and to turn them from darkness to light, and from the power of Satan unto God, that they may receive forgiveness of sins, and inheritance among them which are sanctified by faith that is in me.*
> *—Acts 26:18*

THE GREATEST GIFT IS TO PRAY

Our oldest granddaughter, Sadie, was fixing to graduate from high school in two years. She wanted to get her doctorate in occupational therapy, and I knew that was going to cost her a lot of money. So I started asking the Lord to make a way for her to get into the College of the Ozarks so that she could get her major in psychology and not owe a bundle of money. Now Sadie was and still is a very disciplined young lady if you call age twenty-six young. I do because I see all my grandchildren as my little sweeties. Well, this little sweetie did not know about C of O or "Hard Work U," as most refer to it. All I knew was it was time to start praying and asking God to prepare her heart and for Him to make a way for her to attend that school. I started praying two years before telling her about the school.

Two years passed, and it came time to ask Sadie if she had heard of C of O. She had not heard of the school, so I told her about it and told her she could work her way through with different jobs that the school offered. It was a very disciplined school, and she would receive a very good education there and come out owing very little if any. She wasn't so sure about going there, so I asked her to go to the bank and talk to a friend of mine named Velma Phelan. I asked her to tell Velma how much she thought the total cost of college was going to be and how much she thought Sadie would have to pay a month, and for how many years before it would be paid off.

Now, you can only make suggestions to kids, and then it is their decision whether or not to do as you asked. Come to find out, Sadie did go and talk to Velma and found out what her payment would be, and I guess she thought she might look into C of O after all. She filled out an application, and the next thing I knew, she called me and said she had an interview at the school. I was so excited for her, but that didn't mean she would be accepted, so I kept praying, asking God to direct her path.

The day came for her interview. Her mother went with her, and her Aunt Montana met them at the school for support. I stayed at home because I was not able to take off work at that time, but oh, how I wanted to be there. After the interview, Sadie was told she would find out by letter if she was accepted or not.

It was a long wait, and then the day came, but no letter—or at least I didn't hear from Sadie to tell me she had received one. Two days past the original date, Gary and I were in Jonesboro with our grandsons. We had gone to a John 3:16 event and a Big Daddy Weave concert. After the event, we made a drive through Andy's ice cream, where I received a phone call from Sadie.

She was crying, and I asked her if she was all right.

"I received my letter from C of O, and I got accepted!" she told us through tears.

We were so happy for her, and I still love to thank God for answering those prayers. I also know that it was His will for Sadie to go there, for if it wasn't, God would have put a new desire in my heart. It was not always easy for her; just because it is a Christian school doesn't mean it doesn't have its challenges, but Sadie fought through them all with God's help. He was so very good to her, doing things that I can't even mention. Oh, God is so good.

Sadie graduated with her bachelor of science summa cum laude. She got to go to Belize on a mission trip. She met a lot of good friends and professors. And she learned the value of hard work and the reshaping of her worldviews. She worked at the Keeter Center as bell staff, at the daycare in the three-year-old room, and at the psychology office. Sadie also received the George S. Fry Memorial Award in April 2019, issued by the dean of students. This award was provided by Mr. Paul Fry, class of 1981, in memory of his grandfather. The dean of students chooses the recipients of this award. Selection is from those students who have become aware of themselves as children of God, are eager to earn their way at the college, and will make a contribution to society. She also received the Psychology Outstanding Senior Award, provided and issued by the psychology department faculty in April 2019. It is The Outstanding Senior Award that goes to the highest-ranked psychology major. Sadie truly gives God the glory for all her accomplishments, and so do I.

The greatest gift you can give your grandchildren is to pray for them. I don't care where they are in life or what they are doing—they need someone to pray God's will into their lives. Grandparents' prayers are powerful, God is wonderful, and we are thankful that He hears and answers prayers. Address God with faith; if you feel He is not listening, then maybe you need to take a deep look into your own life and see if there is anything that you need to ask God to remove from your life first through repentance, then walking away from the bondage. Then you can trust God to give you the answer to your prayers. Give Him complete control, for the answer might be yes, no, or wait. Be honest with His answer, and don't falsely change His mind to fit your wants.

"God's Perfect Plan"

God has a perfect plan for our lives
From the beginning to the very end.
Though things may sometimes sadden
His sufficient grace He'll send.
Many questions, of course, will come.
Things may not always seem fair.
But according to His many promises
Our Lord will always be there.
So, really learn to trust Him
Be assured He'll always be near.

Continue to bring Him your problems
He's promised He'll always hear!

Lyle Petersen

Sadie left C of O and entered the Occupational Therapy Doctoral Program at Arkansas State University. She received the Academic Scholar Award, Outstanding Student Award, Phi Kappa Phi Honor Society, and Phi Theta Epsilon. To God be the glory! Thank You, Father God—Sadie knows she could have never accomplished anything without You.

> *Now faith is the substance of things hoped for, the evidence of things not seen.*
> *—Hebrews 11:1*

WHEN THE WALLS START CRASHING IN

Tyler, my great-nephew, was such a sweet little guy growing up. He always got along with his cousins when we all got together. He was also a very smart child. Then the teen years came, and soon the evils of life started hanging around him, changing everything he was. I was made aware of Tyler's actions and changes by my sister Penny, who is Tyler's grandmother. The thought of Tyler going down the wrong path was troubling me. I knew I had to start praying for him because things were getting bad, and I was afraid there might not be a return to normal for him. I started praying for him and asking God to let me know when Tyler might be in danger by putting him on my heart when he needed extra prayer.

There were times I couldn't get Tyler off my mind. I would be working, driving to a client's house, and he would keep popping into my mind, so I would pull off the road and call him. I would tell him he was a good man, and when he was ready for help, there was a program in Poplar Bluff called Crossroads, and my husband Gary and I would try to get him into the program. I would tell him I loved him and was praying for him. He wouldn't say much of anything as I talked, then we would hang up. I would wonder if he really heard anything I was saying or if he even cared. Months would go by, and again Tyler would not leave my mind, so I would call him again, telling him I wanted to help him, and I was praying for him to come to Missouri to get that help. He wouldn't say anything as I talked, but he didn't hang up on me either, so after we would hang up, I would pray that God would put on his heart that I truly cared for him and that he might find hope in what I was saying and consider the chance to get help. He was not himself; he was changing, and it was not just hurting him but it was hurting his family. We all cared so much for him and were scared of what might happen to him if he didn't get help.

One evening, I called Tyler again. I told him that he was going to be surrounded by four walls and that there was not going to be any way out if he didn't get help. I told him he was becoming a person who was not who God intended him to be. I told him again that he was a good man, and I was praying for him to understand just how much he needed to get help.

When I said goodbye, I heard him thinking he had hung up his phone, saying dirty words in anger. I said, "Thank You, Lord; I know you are working in his heart. Please put him in a position where he sees the danger he is in, for he is not our Tyler; he does not know what to do. But, God, You know what it is going to take to bring him to his knees, so please do it quickly—I fear for him."

It wasn't long after that time my sister called and said that Tyler was picked up and put in jail. His family had no idea where he was but came to find out that there was a trailer between their house and where Tyler was staying. Tate, Tyler's brother, just happened to be outside one evening and saw Tyler go into the house. Tate went in and told his dad he saw Tyler going into the house, so Travis, Tyler's father, called the police so they could pick him up. They told Travis they would pick Tyler up if he would not bail him out because that would defeat the purpose. Travis said he wanted Tyler in jail, off the streets, so he at least would know where he was. It was on Father's Day that Travis turned his son in, and it was probably the greatest gift he could have ever received.

Tyler was in jail for eighty-three days until he received a court date, and his family visited him during that time. My sister was so nervous the first time she went to see him. She made a list of things to say so she wouldn't forget. She told him he looked good in orange to break the ice. One thing she knew for sure, she could not even think about posting bail for him.

As days passed slowly for Tyler—not being able to get ahold of drugs, having family visits showing how much they loved him, and time to realize that those four walls were not where he wanted to remain—he wrote me a letter. He was ready to get out and get help, asking if he could get into Crossroads.

I talked to Jimmy, who was over at Crossroads, about Tyler's situation, asking him if Tyler would be eligible to get into the program. He told me he was younger than he actually allowed but to let him know when Tyler was getting out, and he would see what could be done. I gave Travis Jimmy's number to call him when and if the judge would allow Tyler to leave the state of Oklahoma to go to another state to receive help.

On September 11, Tyler went before the judge, who gave him two choices: go back to jail or go to rehab. Travis asked if he could go to rehab in Missouri, and the judge asked when he planned on going. Travis said as soon as you allow us to leave, and that is what they did. Travis took Tyler by to see his grandparents, then off they went. Jimmy had one bed available at Crossroads, which made it possible for Tyler to get help.

God heard our prayers and worked it all out in His time. Tyler went through the program, and he asked the Lord to save him; when he finished Crossroads, he got a job working in concrete. He focused on getting out of debt by paying his school debt and court costs. After a few years, he returned to Oklahoma, got a job working in concrete, and got married. He is back to that sweet guy we have always loved, and his family is united with a new appreciation for one another.

Again, I thank You, Lord, for Your love and guidance when we pray, for our ability to completely depend on You to care and watch over our loved ones when we feel like we have lost them. You are so faithful—may we learn to trust You and praise You for all You do and give You our lives each and every day to do as You will. To God be the Glory. Amen.

> *Rejoice evermore. Pray without ceasing. In everything give thanks: for this is the will of God in Christ Jesus concerning you.*
> *—1 Thessalonians 5:16–18*

When We Are Foolish, He Is Faithful

If only we could turn back time—but oh, what we would have missed out on. I stand in awe when I think of the many foolish things I have done, but God was with me even then. It is hard to grasp just how wonderful and faithful He really is.

He allows you to fail so He can pick you back up again. That is where faith grows, especially when you are basically on your own in raising yourself. My parents were there as far as supplying my basic needs. My mother made sure we were in church, and I know she was a praying woman, but we were never given direction in life. God is real, and you need to believe it—that was about as far as it went.

Now my dad never said twenty-five words to me the whole time I was growing up. It was later in life that we had talks, some good and some not so good. The last seven weeks of his life were probably the closest we ever were. God knew I needed that time with my dad, and I cherish those memories. My mother was the most trusting woman there ever was. If I told her I had choir practice at school until midnight, she believed me. Her main goal in life was to have an immaculate house and for no one to ever see her without makeup. My friends loved her, she loved our friends, and she would always share Jesus with them and listen to their struggles. But she didn't have those special talks with me; it was like I should have all the answers to life, and she needed to get back to cleaning her spotless house. So I was a very free spirit, starting a car hop job at twelve years old so I could make some money, something my dad didn't like handing out. Then I started smoking pot and doing diet pills.

My drug lifestyle continued, and by the time I was eighteen, I had made a choice to get on a bus one morning and go to California. I had to make a change, or I was going to die. I was taking twelve diet pills a day and felt like I was sweating blood. I was sitting in the C&R parking lot at two in the morning and made the decision to go home, pack some clothes, and catch a bus to California. Before I pulled out of the parking lot, I said, "God, if I don't get out of here, I am going to die. I need help." I remember my mother coming into my bedroom as I was packing, and I told her what I was doing. She woke my dad up to stop me, and he said something that I never forgot: "She will be okay—she is the only child we have that can figure someone out in five minutes of being around them."

I went to California, got a job, and got off the diet pills. I enjoyed meeting new people, but I could see and hear the restlessness of a different kind in the hearts of many people. It was very clear that God was not in the lives of most. Back then, in the seventies, homosexuality was everywhere; it was like you were living in another country, something I knew nothing about. People justified it by saying since the Vietnam War, there were seven women to every man. People were living together instead of getting married, and young girls were looking for rich old men, not caring if they were married or not. My eyes were opened to scams going on all the time. God showed me what it was like to live in a cesspool of sin, and I was more aware of sin in my own life for the first time.

Then came the day that a friend and I were going to hitchhike back to Missouri. I was ready to go home. I'd been in California for eighteen months, and I was ready for a calmer way of life. I sold my car to a friend, asked God to help us to have a great trip, and took off hitchhiking back home. The trip was a good one; we received really good rides and made several pit stops along the way to visit friends. Our longest stay was in Louisiana—we stayed a month, enjoying the state and fishing.

When we got back on the road again, we were in Memphis before we knew it. My friend and I had dinner and then decided to get back on the road again, even though it was nine o'clock at night since we were so close to Kennett.

We were on a ramp to get a ride when a semi-truck pulled up. I saw it had three men in the truck, and one of the men got out, offering us a ride. We told him no. He said they had plenty of room. We said no again, and I let the man know I saw three people in the truck.

I started praying, asking God to help us and make the man get back in his truck. All of a sudden, the man grabbed my arm and said, "Let's go."

I jerked my arm away from his grip and said, "Lord, please help me."

Suddenly a state trooper car pulled up with two officers in it. One officer went to the truck, and one officer came to us. I told the officer that the man had grabbed my arm, trying to get us in his truck. This man had said there were only two in his truck, and I told him I saw three and that we did not want to ride with them. The troopers made them leave and then drove us to a restaurant truck stop that was shaped like a barn outside of West Memphis. They told us we could get a safe ride there, and they had a waitress check and see if there was a dependable truck driver going through Kennett.

We were sitting inside drinking coffee when the man who tried to pick me up came in with his friend and sat at a table; then the third man came in, acting like they were long-lost friends. We left our bags outside the entrance, so when the waitress came to our table, I told her that we had already eaten and that we were trying to get to Kennett. I shared how those men tried to pick us up.

"The troopers told me the story," she said. "I will have someone crawl and pick up your bags, and I want you to act like you are going to use the restroom. A truck driver will be waiting on you to take you to Kennett. I will take care of those men."

I know that hitchhiking was not a good move, even though it was done all the time. We had wonderful people pick us up all the way until we got to Memphis. It was chilling when the state troopers told us that two weeks back, a couple was picked up by three men in a semi-truck. They killed the guy and raped the girl, and she dragged herself from where it happened to the road and was rescued the next day. I got very sick to my stomach, knowing there were such sick people in the world.

Even when we get ourselves in a mess, God hears our cries. I have thanked Him over and over, and again right now, for hearing my prayer that night. The truck driver who took us to Kennett took us right up to my friend's brother's door.

All my life, through all my sins, in all my struggles to get it right, You, God, have always had Your hand on me. I now stand in praise of You. I seek Your will for me daily. I get excited for our next journey, and I cannot thank You enough for changing my life. I thank you for Your wisdom and for Your guidance. I thank You for Your holy Word, and I pray that You will correct me if I ever belittle Your power or ability to change the vilest sinner. You gave me Your life, and I owe You mine. Please continue to use me; I am Yours. Make me usable for Your complete glory. Amen.

> *Consequently, he is able to save to the uttermost those who draw near to God through him, since he always lives to make intercession for them.*
> —Hebrews 7:25

> *Even to your old age I am he, and to gray hairs I will carry you. I have made, and I will bear; I will carry and I will save.*
> —Isaiah 46:2

God Help Me

I was driving, and the rain was pouring down where I could hardly see. All of a sudden, I started to hydroplane, and I did not have my seat belt on. I put both hands on the steering wheel to brace myself, both feet on the brake, which I knew not to do, and said, "GOD, HELP ME. I DON'T HAVE ON MY SEAT BELT!" Instantly, I literally felt God put His arms around me tight. I kept my eyes closed but felt the car spinning around and around. The whole time I was calling out to God, asking Him to not let me hurt anyone. All of a sudden, eyes still closed, I hit something big, praying it wasn't a car. I was still feeling the strongest hold around my chest, then I came to a complete stop. I opened my eyes and saw I was off the main road and on the right-of-way. I went to get out of the car, but water started flowing in, so I shut the door and got out on the passenger side. It was still pouring down rain, and I was going to have to walk across a field to call for help and call my Gary.

As I was walking in the pouring rain, I started thinking about the day before. I thought about the night before when I had a headache, and I couldn't get a jug of tea opened because Gary had tightened the lid so tight. Now, I can open any jar that has never been opened, but when Gary tightens a jar, it is impossible for me to open it. So I had to take the pill with water, which I hated to do. The next morning, I was fixing Gary's breakfast and packing his lunch. I got the tea out and tried again to open the lid. Frustrated, I hollered, "Gary Selby!"

He came into the kitchen, and I asked, "HOW MANY TIMES HAVE I ASKED YOU TO NOT TIGHTEN THE JAR LIDS? IF WE

WERE ON THE NEWLYWED GAME AND THEY ASKED YOU WHAT REALLY TICKS ME OFF, WHAT WOULD YOU SAY?"

"Well, you don't like me popping my toes and fingers."

"EXACTLY, AND YOU STILL DO THAT TOO! I HAVE TO WAIT UNTIL YOU GET HOME TO FINISH A MEAL BECAUSE I CAN'T GET THE JARS THAT YOU TIGHTEN OPENED, AND I HAVE ASKED YOU OVER AND OVER AGAIN TO STOP DOING THAT!"

Deflated from my tirade, Gary said, "I think I will go to work where I don't get yelled at," and he walked out the door.

I felt so horrible. I had never yelled at him, and I broke down crying.

So as I was walking through the field to a phone, I thanked God that this accident didn't happen the day before, even though we both apologized when we got home. I told him I was sorry for acting like a crazy woman, and he said he was sorry for tightening the jars over and over again. I thought how awful it would have been if those had been the last words that came out of my mouth before something bad happened to one of us.

I got to the building to call for help and walked back to the car. A police officer was already there, and he called a wrecker for me, and soon Gary arrived. I apologized again for my actions the morning before. When the wrecker got there, the driver and police officer said how lucky I was. They said many had died in that very same spot. When the driver moved the car, there was a cross stuck in the ground right where my car door was. It marked the spot where someone had lost a loved one.

God's arms around me that day humbled me to the core. And Gary's arms around me were just another reason to thank God for His goodness toward me. We are not promised today or tomorrow; let's be careful how we treat the person that God gave us to love and cherish. Let's make sure we do not ignore God and His ultimate presence in our life—He is waiting to make Himself real in your life.

> *For I the Lord thy God will hold thy right hand,*
> *saying unto thee, Fear not; I will help thee.*
> *—Isaiah 41:13*

Acknowledgments

I could not have written these stories if it wasn't for the Lord abiding in my life, saving my soul, and allowing me to experience His presence. It is all for His glory that I declare His greatness.

A special thank you to my husband, Gary. You were always there no matter what my heart was telling me to do, and you did what you could do to help me answer the call. Your patience these last few years as I wrote the stories will never be forgotten. I could not have done this without your support. Thank you so much—I love you!

How could I close this book without thanking my granddaughter Sadie for making sure the stories were sent to the publisher since I am truly computer ignorant. Thank you for supporting me and helping me understand what I had to do to type these stories. Love you, Sweetie!

A BIG THANK YOU to my grandson Easton. I deleted my stories twice, and twice he brought them back to me; a ten-year-old was able to help me! Even Sadie wondered how he retrieved them. Love you, and thank you, Easton.

A heartfelt thank you to Pastor Steve Proctor for his unwavering truth of the Word of God and his desire to feed his flock so they never hunger.

Last but not least are my friends and family who bent their ears and listened to a story to see if it flowed all right. Or listened to their own story to give me the okay on it or to add something they remembered. And a thank you to Beth Lottig for accepting my stories for publication—if only for my family, my heart smiles.

About the Author

Jeanie Selby is married to Gary, her gift from God. She is the thankful mother of two wonderful daughters, J'Anna and Montana, and so blessed that they are married to Wesley and Bryant, two men who love their wives and their children and are very active in their lives. Jeanie is a grandmother of five precious grandchildren: Sadie, Maggie, Jayce, Blaine, and Easton. She has spent the last twenty-three years serving in home health and hospice and literally loved every minute in serving the needs of others. She is now retired and lives with her husband in Wappapello, Missouri, and attends Westwood Baptist Church in Poplar Bluff, Missouri. She loves reading, quilting, cooking, traveling, spending time with her grandchildren, taking walks with her husband, helping others, and telling others about the goodness of God. Jeanie can be contacted by email: selbyjeanie@gmail.com.

www.ingramcontent.com/pod-product-compliance
Lightning Source LLC
Chambersburg PA
CBHW072014110526
44592CB00012B/1309